KEARNEY

Trade wars, pandemics, and chaos

How digital procurement enables
business success in a disordered world

Dr. Elouise Epstein

Foreword by Len DeCandia

KEARNEY

This book is dedicated to my wife, hounds, colleagues, and the procurement community. I feel honored to take this journey with you.

Table of contents

Table of contents (continued)

Foreword

Beyond accelerating the digitization of business processes, the pandemic of 2020/2021 has thrust procurement's practices and value in supplier relationship management to equal footing with customer relationship management. The decades-long struggle for the seat at the table is translating to the need for a seat on the Board, and maybe even advanced competencies in the corner office. Empty shelves, darkened factories, closed borders, and other obstacles have tested global supply chains to their limits. No industry was immune and a time for evaluation and reinvention is upon us. In my current role leading the procurement function in the world's largest healthcare company and after decades of guiding supply management transformations, I found myself challenged by the greatest healthcare and humanitarian crisis of our lifetimes, similar to my many chief procurement officer colleagues. My most recent experience deploying a digital transformation prior to the onset of the pandemic stretched our future-ready infrastructure to an immediate need to be ready now, and we stood the test. We were only able to serve the needs of our many stakeholders in these difficult days by having that future-ready foresight and leveraging the investments comparable to those that you will review in this book.

Through her many experiences and passion and commitment for future readiness, Elouise Epstein captures the shock and impact of the pandemic on the supply chain, specific to sourcing or supply management. She provides an honest and enlightened view on a decades-long, one-dimensional view of procurement and supplier value contributions. Our current times have exposed the critical need for investment in enabling technologies, advanced practices, and most importantly, staff competencies in digital literacy that elevates data analytics and insight-driven decision-making. Elouise and I share many common experiences in her 20-plus years as a consultant and collaborator for Kearney. For me over the past 25 years, I have been in the role of either the chief procurement or supply officer for four exceptional Fortune 100 companies. These assignments have included the deployment of next generation technologies, commensurate with embedding practices and shaping elevated competencies that have delivered measurable P&L contributions. Elouise's book will inspire you to ignite and press on with your plans and actions for change, regardless of where you are in your transformational journey. Leadership resides in all organizations irrespective of title. The great responsibility of leadership is to anticipate and prepare for the future, or as our world has painfully shown us, for the unexpected.

This book is a transparent and fearless view of pre-pandemic obstacles or the many "villains" that have hindered progress for the procurement function. It provides an opportunity for you to evaluate the reality of your current environment with a critical, honest assessment. Elouise educates and builds on the transformational advancement of cloud-based technological tools that provides freedom to supply management from the heavy and rigid ERP technologies holding back an agile and resilient supply base. She educates the reader on the pallet of technological choices which help to build a people, process, and automation plan that will guide and position you for your team's "hero" journey of the procurement function and organization-wide supply management competencies that will allow you to be valued contributors to all of your business stakeholders. The stakeholder community has expanded dramatically beyond the single-minded view of profit or savings. Procurement has the distinct opportunity to be reframed and repositioned as an essential hub for your organization's ESG (environment, social, and governance) strategy. Moving beyond protecting your company's brand or image, supply management practices in diverse supplier strategies can help drive positive social impact outcomes. Visible and leading practices in citizenship and sustainability can be amplified through your supply base by elevating expectations and sharing best practices with investment in mentoring. The 21st century procurement team recognizes that their stakeholder community goes beyond customers and shareholders: it includes all your fellow employees, your supplier's employees, and their respective communities.

Expanding procurement's role and influence in an effective and efficient way requires a step change in competencies and skills that are discussed in the later sections of the book. Investment in the development of talent and engagement of that talent to make the function a destination or critical development assignment for future leaders is a legacy for all current CPOs and their leadership teams. Exceptional foundational competency in category and supplier management must be supplemented with business skills in financial analysis, partner engagement, and empathy capabilities that include active listening, storytelling, innovative thinking, and persistence in driving change.

Elevating the engagement model both internally and externally to valued partner status is dependent upon two fundamental pillars: trust and competency. Trust, or respect, is earned one drop at a time and can be lost in gallons, so every engagement at all levels of your teams is important. Having your team aligned on a common vision of the future and an honest assessment of current state is an outcome of following the methodology of plan development outlined in this book. Establishing a common vocabulary, facing into and dismantling roadblocks with a strong commitment of bringing every one of your stakeholders along with you is fundamental to success. Your personal commitment to being a lifelong learner through the experiences and insights shared by Elouise is an affirmation of your personal commitment to growth and development. A leader should role-model these behaviors of investing in their personal growth. Even after 40 years in industry, I have always considered myself to be curious and restless, always open to new thinking.

Similarly, circumstances have positioned you in our chosen profession to use these insights to make a difference; as supply management professionals and leaders we can and must use these tragic times to make the world a better place.

In closing, this book challenges you to evaluate your perspective. Elouise, with her forward-thinking insights and practices, embodies the perspective of a "futurist." My many experiences during times of crisis, growth, and change within industry would most likely classify me as a "realist." Reading this book and shaping a plan that best addresses the culture and business climate of your situation will allow you to be an "optimist." A unique window in time to be aware, inspired, and motivated to create a future of contribution and experience beyond what you had hoped in your chosen profession.

Allow me to share a personal experience in creating an environment of partnering. Over 20 years ago I was the Founding Chair of the Rutgers University Center for Supply Chain Management, a role I maintained for 12 years before accepting my current position on the Rutgers Business School Advisory Board. At that time, we were still in the early days of the science of supply chain management and it was an opportunity to build a place of collaboration for my industry colleagues and invest in future leaders. It continues to be a humbling experience to see that the supply chain management program at Rutgers University is the second largest program in the US and is recognized as a global leader by Gartner and others. This is an example of one of my proudest legacies.

What Elouise presents in this book may be your opportunity to create your own personal legacy that pushes our profession forward. I believe you are capable and you should take on this challenge. You are positioned as collaborative procurement leaders to invest in the tools that will deliver the ability to scale solutions that will drive positive business, environmental, and social outcomes that will make the difference our world needs. Let's learn and work together to build a future that is better from the experiences and learnings of this dreadful pandemic.

Len DeCandia

Princeton, New Jersey
Current Global Chief Procurement Officer – Johnson & Johnson
Former Chief Procurement Officer – The Estée Lauder Companies Inc.
Former Chief Supply Officer – AmerisourceBergen Corporation
Former Chief Supply Officer – Roche Pharmaceuticals North America

Acknowledgments

This book would not have been possible without the generous contributions of many people.

First, I would like to thank Len DeCandia for contributing such a gracious and thoughtful foreword in addition to critical feedback on the manuscript. I am both thrilled and honored to receive his insights, guidance, and mentorship. I am equally grateful to Jeff Hewitt, Tiffany Hickerson, Gillis Jonk, Arshita Raju, and Bill Frazier for contributing material to this book.

Also, a sincere thank you to Richard Williams from PSG, Mike Cadieux from Procurement Foundry, Rajesh Kalidindi from LevaData, Joel Hyatt, Jared Hyatt, and Keith Hausmann from Globality, Ben Winter from Fairmarkit, and Cyril Pourrat and Adam Brown from BT Sourced, all of whom granted me a behind-the-scenes look into their operations.

My sincere gratitude to my colleagues Ana Conde, Tom Kline, Joel Saldana, Lynne McDonnell, Shakil Nathoo, Prasad Poruri, Vishal Bhandari, Carol Cruickshank, and Jane Wanklyn for their intellectual partnership and collaboration. Emily Deng deserves a special award for helping to organize both me and everything that went into this book.

I would like to recognize the contributions of Kristin Boswell, Haley Dunbrack, Briana Flosi, Chaillé Biddle, Kerry MacKenzie, and the Kearney production team for breathing life into this book and getting it ready for the world. A special thank-you to John Blascovich for coaching and championing me throughout this entire process and to Mark Clouse, Steve Mehltretter, and

Fred Eng for their financial support in bringing this book to life. Similarly, my sincere gratitude to Kearney Partner Emeritus Joe Raudabaugh without whose support I would not have had this extraordinary career.

I would like to recognize John Clayton for editing and helping to bring this manuscript to a level of readable clarity.

I am immensely grateful to Sheila Gulati, Mike Schiappa, and Paul Martyn for their reading and commenting.

I am indebted to Jan Fokke van den Bosch, Brian Smith, Julian Hooks, Heidi Landry, Shashi Mandapaty, Anthony Adeleye, Bill Gunn, Sally Macaluso, and Jim Martin, for the opportunity to partner together in developing the future.

I am thankful to Donna Wilczek, Stephany Lapierre, Amanda Prochaska, and Sarah Scudder for their inspiration, sparring, and friendship. A special mention goes to my public speaking coach Sarah Elovich who has helped me shape and refine this material.

Of course, no list of recognition would be complete without giving significant credit to my lovely wife Denise whose support has been and continues to be beyond measure. Also, a special mention for our hound brigade who ensure I get out into nature, where many ideas come to light.

Finally, I would like to thank my former colleague and collaborator Stephen Easton for investing, challenging, and helping to bring to fruition the vision of a better procurement.

Background

"No plan survives first contact"

Helmuth von Moltke, Prussian military commander[1]

During a workshop in November 2019, a retail chief purchasing officer (and client) bragged to me about not needing inventory optimization. This executive's organization had "next-day delivery with our suppliers," I was told. They could get whatever they needed in 24 hours.

Four months later, in the middle of the pandemic, I didn't hear anyone bragging about the benefits of just-in-time.

As the COVID-19 crisis hit its first US spike in March 2020, it became nearly impossible for most businesses, including our retail CPO, to find sufficient personal protective equipment (PPE). Demand far outpaced supply. This same retail purchasing organization sought Kearney's help to source PPE. We were happy to oblige. Employing our best sourcing capabilities, we managed to secure a decent-sized supply. When we presented our results, the client said that the cost was three times the approved threshold for PPE. Additional approvals were required. Thirty-six hours later, those approvals were secured—but the PPE was no longer available.

[1] The actual quotation is "No plan of operations reaches with any certainty beyond the first encounter with the enemy's main force." Susan Ratcliffe, Editor, *Oxford Essential Quotations*, Oxford University Press, online version, 2016, https://www.oxfordreference.com/view/10.1093/acref/9780191826719.001.0001/q-oro-ed4-00007547

I was sad, but not surprised. I watched variations of this story repeat over and over. Procurement organizations continually failed in their ability to secure PPE, hand sanitizer, janitorial services, video teleconferencing services, and all kinds of other indirect items that became major roadblocks to daily operations during the pandemic. I watched companies throw internal people and external consultants at the problem. Over the coming months, thanks to a great deal of hard work, my client and many other organizations weathered the crisis.

But the damage was done—damage to the old-fashioned ways of doing procurement. Everything we'd been told about procurement best practices, processes, talent, technology, and data was at best a fallacy. At worst it had all been outright lies. Twenty years of blind focus on cutting costs and controlling spend caught up with the procurement function.

Before the pandemic, I wanted to write this book as a how-to for digital procurement with a nod toward the future. It would be a guide to the basics of what digital procurement is, from a theoretical and practical point of view. It would explain how to deploy, design, and operate systems in preparation for the procurement organization of the future. COVID-19 eviscerated that intention. I predicted that the future was a freight train heading toward us, but well off in the distance. I was wrong: the train was right in front of us. It hit us full force. The impact did more than highlight weaknesses in procurement organizations— it exacerbated them exponentially. Lack of visibility into spend and/or suppliers, lack of supplier identification, lack of a broader community, lack of capabilities, and lack of leadership all became examples of procurement done poorly. In an instant, the pandemic proved that old operating models need to be ripped up and tossed aside—not at some vague point in the future, but as soon as possible. In their place, a new *digital-first* procurement organization must emerge.

Over the past decade, many organizations spent a great deal of money on procurement transformations—and their efforts weren't adequate in preparing for COVID-19. Who was to blame? The strategists or those charged with enacting the strategies? The answer has never mattered. Maybe the strategies were too complex, too theoretical. Maybe the people weren't up to the task. Or maybe the technology was inadequate. Maybe all of this is true. Nevertheless, unassailably, going forward, we need to do something *different*. That different is what this book is about. It's a how-to for building a *procurement operations model* that will withstand the next major disruption.

Why should you listen to me? Here's why. I am truly independent. I do not take money or any other compensation from any vendor. I am a strategic advisor for my clients. I have a vested interest in every recommendation. How my clients use any technology that I recommend is part of my investment in every client where I make a suggestion. I stand behind my work and help clients adjust their strategies as they go, based on how their vendors are performing, or failing to perform. So I get a fully completed feedback loop.

I am constantly amazed that vendors pay independent entities to rate them. How silly! Organizations should be able to make that evaluation for themselves.

I have particular expertise in procurement start-ups. I chart the disruptions they create. When I talk to founders, clients, or venture capitalists (VCs), I take no remuneration of any sort. I pay for lunches and dinners so that there is never a conflict of interest. When I am asked to speak, they know that I am going to be uncensored and unfiltered. I will go after anyone and everyone, especially consultants.

I'm a huge advocate for these start-ups. I believe in what the founders are trying to do—to make the work of procurement tasks efficient, or even cool. I'm excited for the transformation they're bringing to the procurement function. I want to elevate their voices and, in the process, help our industry thrive.

This story is about digital procurement and the future, but I won't be using terms such as *artificial intelligence* (AI), *machine learning* (ML), *robotic process automation* (RPA), *blockchain*, or *Internet of Things* (IoT). For our purposes, these are nonsense words, because they are mere enablers. When I set out to write this book, I didn't start with the features of word processing software packages or the esoteric rules of grammar—instead I articulated the vision of what I wanted to do, and allowed that vision to dictate the tools and team-mates I would use to accomplish it. Likewise, as a procurement professional, what you need to do is set up a vision and allow that strategy to dictate the enabling technologies you will buy.

Each section is structured with personal commentary and background so that you can see how the insights emerged. I have included anecdotes throughout to contextualize what is happening against historical trends. If we can highlight our collective failures, we can better achieve the goal of building a new path forward. I want to get rid of *business as usual*. I want to throw out all of our existing assumptions and "best practices," not because I think they're wrong (although I do) but because they are based on patently old logic, as was exposed during the pandemic. Nobody is safe from criticism, not even my colleagues. If my style seems overly caustic, know that it arises from frustration: I feel we have an opportunity right now to do great work. But if we don't snap out of collective stupor, we'll miss that opportunity, and procurement will be forever relegated to the role of budget enforcement. I will go to extremes to try to snap you out of that stupor.

I have the greatest job in the world. I get to do what I love—talking to people. I talk to CPOs, vendors, analysts, consultants, VCs, start-up founders, and pretty much anybody who will talk to me. This affords me tremendous access to what people are thinking, and how they are thinking it. What I do is distill it down, extract implications, and look at bigger-picture issues. Then, I get to act on what I hear from these conversations. I help clients leapfrog to the future or, if necessary, remediate and then leapfrog. This is very gratifying. I started in this field 21 years ago, so I have seen this entire industry emerge and evolve; I have lived it. This ability to look at trends over time gives me a useful view into what is working, what is not, and what we can hope will happen.

I started writing this book in early March 2020, at the start of quarantine. As I wrote the book and COVID-19 shifted the world, the lessons became clear. For example, now that so much has been accomplished, working from home will become much more of a standard—and the old ways of work (the *best-in-class* frameworks and processes) will be even more obviously inadequate to their tasks.

But 2020 was remarkable not only for the COVID crisis. Sadly, that stress was mixed with the volatility of unrelenting racist actions against Black people, with a flash point around the murder of George Floyd. Citizens, companies, and governments realized they needed to do more, to do better. Building a just society is not only about making virtuous tweets, but also about changing practices. And the procurement function, with its impact on third-party spend, is well situated to turn words into on-the-ground actions.

Some people like to be provocative just to be provocative. They're lazy and they've realized that being a contrarian is easy. I'm trying to be provocative because I truly believe in the disruption that's happening. This is *good* disruption, which will lead to a better world. I will provide evidence of how it's playing out.

I am also trying to be provocative because my job gives me a unique platform, an opportunity to push us forward. My opinions are not always popular, but they're based on thousands of hours of continual conversations with procurement's best and brightest at all levels, and on various strategy projects. My goal is not to pick the best of the best; my goal is to illustrate the art of the possible. My sincere hope and belief is that people in every organization can do their own evaluations and no longer need to rely on consultants or analysts.

At the Scout SPARK conference in February 2020, I said, "Now is the greatest time to be in procurement." I still believe that—even more so since the pandemic.

You can look at COVID-19 positively or negatively. The negative view is that the pandemic proved that all our best-in-class frameworks, templates, and maturity models were inadequate. They did have some value, just not the promised value. That's why so many "leaders" struggled so much during the crisis. The positive view is that COVID-19 is giving us an opportunity to redesign how we do procurement.

We are on a journey to reimagine procurement. In literary terms, we are embarking on the hero's journey. As such, there will be villains, challenges, and rewards. At the end of the journey, we will be transformed. The first of the book's three sections identifies our challenges and villains. Despite the directness of the tone, this is not to castigate anybody in particular. The goal here is to depict the pitfalls of the past so that we can properly orient ourselves. I go into detail about these obstacles because they are part of today's reality. And, even if we overcome these hurdles and capture the villains of the procurement world, there are still many real-world elements that reside outside of our control (e.g. company culture, state of the business, timing, skillsets, and so on). Thus, the second section focuses on providing the tools and directions to operate in this reality and at the same time take a journey to the future. Coming out of the current pandemic opportunity is everywhere, especially as we leverage the vast innovation in the digital world around us. This part explains how to harness the power of digital and start to effect the change we want to see. The third section illustrates the outcome of our transformation. It shows us a view of what is possible when we take this journey. In that spirit, this book is for the next generation of procurement practitioners, leaders, consultants, technology providers, and community.

Introduction

Digital tools have fundamentally changed the way that business operates today. We see this transformation in sales. We see it in engineering. We see it in the fundamental ways of working generated by the pandemic—many executives now operate from home, taking advantage of digital tools. But we don't see this transformation in procurement.

This lack of digital adoption is of particular concern because procurement is rapidly becoming one of the most crucial capabilities in today's enterprise. The function has grown in strategic importance, moving from simple back-office cost savings generators to one that is part and parcel of executing the vital agenda of innovation, environmental, social, and governance (ESG), supply assurance, and new third-party business models. As companies have externalized much of their operations, procurement increasingly plays a critical role in the successful engagement and orchestration of the third-party environment. As such, it has become a destination of choice for visionary leaders and high-performing employees who seek to engage in purpose-driven work. Naturally, digital is the critical enabler of all of this value-driven work.

Why has digital not made its way to procurement? The problem may go back several decades, to the traditional, unfair view of procurement as unsexy. For too long, procurement was seen as a backwater, a place to store your least productive employees—a function with little potential to add value to the enterprise. That view is mostly changed now, but its legacy can have surprising effects.

More proximately, we might blame today's technology vendors and the vast apparatus of analysts, consultants, and industry groups that supports those vendors. They have not given us the digital tools that can bring about this transformation.

On the other hand, we as procurement professionals have not demanded those tools. At heart, the problem is one of vision. Procurement leaders must believe in a digital future. We must believe, first, that good digital tools will accomplish a meaningful transformation, and second, that this transformation will bring meaningful value to the enterprise. If we don't hold these beliefs, how can we expect others—within our organizations, or among those vendors—to do so?

This book is about that vision and that potential. I believe that with digital tools slashing through bureaucracy, procurement can accomplish its current functions with, say, 30 percent of its current resources. But I do not envision a diminished future. Rather, I believe that digital tools can also help procurement expand its role in creating value. The heart of any enterprise—whether it's simple or complex, manufacturing or services, B2B or B2C, large or small—involves taking inputs, transforming them, and selling that product in ways that improve customers' lives. In today's complex and sophisticated global marketplace, *getting better inputs* may be the biggest lever we have to make a greater difference.

That lever operates with digital tools. This book will show you how.

Today is the greatest time to be in procurement

The procurement function stands at the precipice of a new decade that will be punctuated by endless macro disruptions, massive technological innovation, and a new generation of professionals. It's an era of uncertainty. Institutions created after World War II (such as the United Nations, North American Treaty Organization, and European Union) long provided a stable operating and legal foundation on which to conduct business, but those institutions are now imperiled. Indeed, governments and global institutions once addressed intellectual property protection, R&D, security, financial stability, and risk—but now businesses likely must put greater efforts into all these areas. As COVID-19 demonstrated, businesses need to build extensible, flexible, and resilient supply chains that can adapt locally or globally based on changing political and economic conditions. Yet it's a challenging time to work in operations, because many enterprises seem more focused today on the commercial side of their business, in pursuit of earnings targets and short-term profit.

Nevertheless, the procurement profession has matured from people who simply ended up there to a new generation of motivated, highly capable difference-makers. When I think of *procurement professionals*, I imagine people like Jennifer, the 28-year-old business athlete who secured her seat at the product development table and makes daily cost/quality/sustainability trade-offs for all new-product designs. I think of Danielle, who's not afraid of technology and analytics, and who actively seeks to improve processes and user experience. Jennifer and Danielle have different traits and skills than the procurement professionals who came before them. They're unencumbered by the past and not afraid to ask, "Why are we doing it this way?" They don't accept mediocrity and are willing to point out alternative ways of doing business. For example, they recognize the need for their companies to work with start-ups and universities—and they also recognize that in a small company, a risk-averse corporate *supplier onboarding process* would crush the opportunity to pursue those creative relationships. This is a challenge that Jennifer or Danielle would tackle without hesitation. Increasingly they are being asked to think in the context of both bottom-line savings and top-line growth—while also ensuring a socially just, environmentally friendly, and resilient source of supply. Jennifer and Danielle appreciate, and will lobby to expand, the direct line from procurement to the consumer. They expect and even welcome the idea that supply disruptions, ingredients, quality, and risk should factor into their individual performance. More importantly, it is easy to see that they represent the next generation of procurement and will be the inspirational leaders of tomorrow.

Incidentally, this new generation is hyper-networked and prone to collective success beyond the four walls of an individual enterprise. They no longer see business as a zero-sum game of information-hoarding, posturing, and arrogance. Part of this change can be attributed to the fact that procurement organizations are far more diverse and inclusive than they have ever been in the past. This internal change of generations and cultures—as much as external events such as hurricanes or pandemics—should be prompting leaders to question whether traditional "best practices" and "best-in-class" templates remain relevant.

Surprisingly, manual processes still dominate today's procurement organizations. They're like white-collar versions of 1970s manufacturing facilities, with legions of people handling low-value activities—in this case, sourcing and demand management. Time and attention are consumed by routine, labor-intensive transactional activities such as pricing negotiations, contract awards, and supplier performance monitoring. Procurement workers spend hours piecing together fragmented information flows from myriad transactions—a task that technology could perform in seconds. Indeed, automation has transformed other business functions. So internal stakeholders from those functions grow frustrated by what they perceive as slow service from procurement. They yearn for self-service options and direct access to more comprehensive information about the purchasing process. And procurement should be able to satisfy them: digital technologies are on pace to automate and create transparency for most routine processes within three to five years. Of course, such a prediction assumes that the procurement function will embrace these new digital technologies.

Customers are always the biggest drivers of change. Books, articles, and news reports are continually highlighting the changing demographics and habits of consumers. Today's consumers increasingly consist of a younger, more socially conscious generation who expect businesses to take a greater role in the solving of (rather than contributing to) the world's biggest problems. In response, procurement and supply chain operations need to address these ever-changing customer preferences by embracing the era of hyper-transparency. Thus, companies need to make good on ESG. Most ESG programs are inadequate; at best they're a check-the-box marketing activity. Tomorrow's supply chains will need to put environmental impact front *and* center. Consumers are increasingly demanding it, and governments will too. Most people can see that global climate change is real and that it's having tangible impacts. People have less tolerance for the destruction of native habitats to produce cheap palm oil, or the burning of rainforests to produce beef, or the slaughtering of animals in factories, or the torture of bees to produce honey. Individual consumers can't avoid these issues as they permeate the collective consciousness via social media. These concerns thus affect how products get packaged and delivered—and, most importantly, from whom they are sourced. Procurement experts need to be ahead of these trends.

Indeed, once the COVID-19 crisis abates, sustainability will resume its focus as a core business objective for most companies. As such, procurement will be on the front lines of developing and achieving these objectives. That's because these objectives are tied to the company's entire value chain—which means that procurement can be the focal point for a wide variety of opportunities.

Ultimately, the world is moving to more micro, on-demand-based economies. To see how painful supply disruption can be, you need look no further than recent tariffs, or natural disasters in Puerto Rico, or predictions about Brexit. Coming years will see more and more of these disruptions and challenges. Given the decline of transnational institutions such as the United Nations and European Union, businesses must put greater efforts into their own intellectual property (IP) protection, R&D, security, and financial stability. Thus, building and operating a supply chain in the future will become both more complicated and more crucial. It will require businesses to build extensible, flexible, and resilient supply chains that can adapt to be local or global as political and economic conditions change.

In short, procurement is about to change dramatically for the good. That change will ensure that the function becomes a strategic imperative for all corporations. The saying "Past performance is not indicative of future results" was invented by lawyers to abjure responsibility for failure. In the case of procurement, the saying will soon refer to increased responsibility and success.

The problem

However, the promise of procurement is stymied by many current problems. Section I will investigate these problems and their causes, but to set the scene, let's acknowledge that procurement is currently being held back by factors including:

1 **Doing budget control rather than value creation.** I will return continually to this theme because it's so important to the procurement vision. The easy way to do procurement is to be a budget enforcer. "Procurement succeeded because our manufacturing inputs came in under budget." "We should budget paperclips at $0.005 apiece." "We can't pay that much

for PPE." When procurement is a shadow budget organization, it is indeed a backwater. It is not in control of its destiny. It is not adding value. As budget controls become increasingly digitized—which they should—procurement is diminished almost to the point of nonexistence.

2 **Decades of cost squeezing.** That budgetary mindset coexists with a mindset that equates *value* with *lowest price*. As the pandemic showed, a heedless pursuit of low cost can lead to low resilience—in other words, it can set the enterprise up for failure amid crisis. Procurement is responsible for *relationships* with suppliers, and those relationships need to go beyond cost to include factors such as innovation, resilience, and value creation.

3 **Lack of data flow.** Data flow is a problem for many business functions. Data always seems to exist in inconvenient silos. This is especially important for procurement, with its reliance on data about your company's inputs and the suppliers of those inputs. This is data not only about costs, but also the other relationship factors mentioned above.

4 **Outdated business practices.** In addition to the cost focus and siloed data, procurement is home to plenty of other outdated business practices, such as the overemphasized distinction between *directs* and *indirects*, industry groups that sell contact information, and an overreliance on manual labor. Most importantly, procurement has an outdated view of technology: it focuses on end-to-end solutions rather than digital platforms.

5 **Brittle systems.** As a result of these outdated practices, procurement is surprisingly brittle—capable of breaking at the smallest provocation. Something far smaller than a worldwide pandemic would have also caused havoc in 2020. Yet other functions—such as consumer distribution of e-commerce products—proved far more resilient.

6 **Limited environmental, social, governance.** Because procurement systems were built for a previous generation's priorities, they do not adapt well as those priorities change. As today's consumers demand increased attention to issues including the environment and social justice, corporate leaders agree—and yet procurement is stuck without a good way to implement essential initiatives.

In short, we live in a changing world. And procurement is making an inadequate response to change. Yet the response to that situation should not be, "Try harder!" Procurement people are already trying hard, but they're laboring in a system that too often is not structured to *let* them respond to change.

That's why it's so important for procurement to not merely "go digital." Laying digital processes atop these flawed structures will be ineffectual at best. Procurement needs to examine and reset its core foundations to take advantage of the best that digital technologies have to offer.

Why? Because the pace of change will only increase.

The future: massive disruptions

It's tempting to say that COVID-19 was a surprise crisis, *just the beginning* of a more uncertain future; in fact, massive disruptions are the reality of our world. Since 2000, there have been the 9/11 terrorist attacks, eight of the most destructive hurricanes on record, four of the most devastating earthquakes, two of the most destructive tsunamis, cyberattacks (including the massive Russian attack on US government systems), wildfires, one enormous financial meltdown, and of course pandemics. Some people call this the "new normal"— although my colleagues at Kearney prefer to call it the No Normal, because there will be nothing normal about it. Furthermore, as the list above shows, these disruptions are not even representative of the new normal but of the old normal. Cataclysmic events are not aberrations. The fact that we pretend they are out of the ordinary is a human blind spot and wishful thinking.[1]

Instead the cataclysms represent the new realities in which businesses will have to operate. What will happen when (sadly, not *if*) the world gets hit with

[1] Hurricanes: Yolanda 2013, Usagi 2013, Nicole 2016, Igor 2010, Sandy 2012, Olga 2001, Karl 2004, Morakot 2009, Jennifer Jones, "10 Largest Hurricanes Ever Recorded," June 1, 2019, https://largest.org/nature/hurricanes/
Tsunamis: Sumatra, Indonesia, December 26, 2004; North Pacific Coast, Japan, March 11, 2011, Campbell Phillips, "The 10 most destructive tsunamis in history," *Australian Geographic*, March 16, 2011, https://www.australiangeographic.com.au/topics/science-environment/2011/03/the-10-most-destructive-tsunamis-in-history/
Earthquakes: Sumatra, Indonesia, March 28, 2005 (8.6); *Bio bio Chile*, February 27, 2010 (8.8); Sendai, Japan, March 11, 2011 (9.0); Sumatra, Indonesia, December 26, 2004 (9.1), Campbell Phillips, "Earthquakes: the 10 biggest in history," *Australian Geographic*, March 14, 2011, https://www.australiangeographic.com.au/topics/science-environment/2011/03/earthquakes-the-10-biggest-in-history/

a massive cyberattack? That could create the same kind of chaos that COVID-19 has brought with it. In the post-pandemic world, we face unprecedented dislocation at the government, corporate, and individual levels. Simultaneously, significant countries worldwide are experiencing mounting geopolitical risks, currency volatility, unbalanced economic growth, and trade and investment uncertainties. As if these daunting realities were not enough, environmental degradation continues to be a profoundly serious longer-range concern.

Given that these disruptions are here to stay, and new ones are coming, is procurement ready? Are we looking forward? Are we anticipating and planning for future disruptions? Are we adaptable to the change that is coming? The trade wars of the late 2010s caught the business world largely unprepared, as companies had to undertake crash efforts to figure out which parts and suppliers were affected by the tariffs. Given that tariffs may return, does procurement now have good data that can better address such crises next time? In fact, given that this dynamic plays out every hurricane season, every typhoon season, every fire season—potentially every month of the year—does procurement have systems that will allow for smart responses? Typically, we respond by throwing people at the problem, and then the problem passes, and we walk away and go back to "normal." Embracing digital technologies will help us respond to these issues much more efficiently. We will be able to do forward-planning so that we aren't caught flat-footed when the next major disruption hits.

Initial lessons from COVID-19

It will take decades to fully process the impacts and implications of the pandemic. Historians, political scientists, and other researchers will likely debate the causes, government reactions, and questions of who knew what and when. However, it doesn't take a historian to deduce immediate learnings from this crisis. The traditional procurement process—the "best-in-class" process—was exposed as totally fraudulent. The highly structured, linear-based, rigid procurement process wasn't up to the task. Was it already under strain in trying to adapt to the realities of business operations in the 21st century? Sure, but then the pandemic hit it like a torpedo smashing the broad side of a non-reinforced metal hull.

As the crisis became apparent to the world, it was genuinely sad to see how many companies struggled to get basic visibility into its impact on their supply base. They lacked visibility into where their suppliers were, how much and what spend resided with those suppliers, who were alternative suppliers, and how financially stable suppliers were to withstand the crisis. Vendors did step in—and employees and communities stepped up—to soften the worst blows for many companies. But how could the collective industry have been so ill-prepared?

The pandemic also exposed *risk modeling* as totally fraudulent. All consultants, risk managers, and risk solution providers should be ashamed of themselves. How many consultants factored pandemics into their risk modeling? How many risk managers had business continuity plans for a pandemic? How many risk monitoring solutions had pandemic as a *view*? How many sourcing awards truly factored risk profile as part of the award? How many suppliers were flagged during the onboarding process? The answer to all these questions is *very little*—and those that did do something failed to go far enough. The enterprises that recovered quickly and found some level of operating capability throughout this crisis did so not because of their processes, models, or tools—they did so by the pure grit, determination, and skill of their employees. (That and 100,000 Zoom meetings.) The way to survive the pandemic was to ignore service-level agreements (SLAs), compliance, and cost controls. If you're desperate for PPE to keep your facility open, you will pay a premium—which is not a procurement best practice. If during a pandemic you find only one bid, you may violate your procurement best practice of three bids and a buy. Adhering to contracted SLAs will likewise slow your response in a disaster. In a crisis response, you have to be flexible. You need not only dedicated people but also an agile approach. In other words, there's no best practice or manual to follow during a crisis.

To be fair to those in the risk game, their tepid risk modeling reflected broader business objectives that put maximizing profit and minimizing cost above everything else. Advocates of just-in-time supply chains could not even imagine a scenario they could possibly face that would require stockpiles of equipment and supplies. As a result, risk managers were not empowered to do anything that impeded operations or diminished profits. Risk technology vendors deserve some blame for producing tepid risk monitoring that tells the user almost nothing of value. But there's no excuse for consultants—our job is to push our clients to make the tough decisions. If and when they don't, we have very public platforms to challenge the collective industry.

Let me explain with some personal perspectives: although I myself am a consultant—doing work that I love at a firm full of wonderful people—I do believe in shining a light into the dark, unspoken areas of consulting. All too often, people see consultants as arrogant, expensive, tone-deaf, and disconnected from reality—even if what we're doing proves to be spot-on. Sometimes we're wrong, because nobody's perfect. In general, we should have better attitudes about this, and I certainly try. But what I can't stand is when consultants charge large fees for work that is *patently* wrong. This includes almost all previous procurement technology consulting.

In the *nobody's perfect* category, every consultant that was hired to do a cost-savings project over the past five years participated in the trend to over-index on cost at the expense of supply assurance. But at Kearney, we believe that consulting is about being a *trusted advisor*. So, I will acknowledge here and now: all of us should have spent much more time in the past five years talking about pandemics in risk modeling. We should have done better at challenging the status quo. I regret that we didn't. But now I am using this public platform to try to do so—because the pandemic has made clear that *continuing* to ignore resilience (supplier diversity, sustainability, innovation, and other non-cost savings initiatives) would be patently wrong.

COVID-19 taught us that procurement organizations were far too fragile and far too focused on controlling spend. They should instead have focused on value-generating activities that genuinely contribute to the enterprise. This crisis required procurement to have real-time insights, and work cross-category and cross-value chain, with little or no focus on cost. When you need transportation now and you're competing with a hundred other companies for the same resource, *spend management* goes flying out the window.

Undoubtedly a new procurement organization operating model will emerge, replete with agile processes, sophisticated technology, and useful insights. These issues surfaced during previous natural disasters, but those were always localized and overcome with brute force and a little bit of ignorance, plus a lot of human intervention. For example, when President Donald Trump enacted tariffs in late 2018, how many procurement organizations scrambled to figure out the impact on their cost to produce? How many could report instantaneously on the impact, and do scenario modeling or reallocation?

It should have been easy for procurement organizations to plug in projected cost increases and model the impact across every bill of materials (BoM) to produce a set of implications and new strategies. Furthermore, as we'll argue later, this should have been automated. Instead, the world experienced a global disruption and discovered that operating models, processes, and technology were not up to the task.

COVID-19 also taught us that historical demand-based models are wholly inadequate for informing a crisis response. When entire segments of a supply chain break down, along with the constraints placed around consumer demand, traditional models lack the necessary data to be effective. Similarly, we learned that the distinction between directs (materials that go into the product being produced or service delivered) and indirects (goods and services not directly incorporated into the end product or service) is outdated. In a crisis, almost everything becomes a precious commodity, even hand sanitizer and videoconferencing software.

The most vivid threat of socialism has always been that government central planning will fail to feed people, fail to provide adequate consumer products. But during the pandemic, we learned that Amazon, Instacart, UPS, and FedEx are the true central planners of our society. They decided who got what goods, and when. At the height of the crisis, Amazon and Instacart throttled demand to ensure equitable distribution of products and prevent hoarding. For CPG companies, this distribution throttling tangibly disrupts forecasts and supply planning. This is a new dynamic for supply chains to have to account for.

Perhaps all this can be summed up with one crucial lesson: going forward, *best-in-class* will be *risk-optimized* supply chains. Because now we know the risks are coming, and we have at least a vague sense of the damage they can do.

What's all this "digital" nonsense?

Digital exploded into the collective business lexicon in the late 2010s. Like so many other buzzwords, it lacked a clear definition or common understanding. When we say *digital*, do we mean the digitizing of paper processes? Do we mean the adoption of digital tools? Do we mean changing fundamental processes and making them digital? All of the above? Something else?

At a theoretical level, any of that sounds good. Who doesn't want to be digital? It's so 21st century. And so many organizations, goosed by consultants' PowerPoint slides, are undertaking "digital transformations." But few people can articulate what such a transformation means for individual functions. Nowhere is this more evident than in procurement. It's silly to arbitrarily cast a *digital* net over procurement. Instead, we need to talk about the details of what will become digital and how.

Simply defined, *digital procurement* applies sophisticated technology and insights to a company's need to procure goods and services in order to create value. That's the goal: creating more value by applying better insights. Although subsequent sections will provide detailed examples, for the sake of illustration, here are some brief summaries of basic examples of good digital procurement:

— Reducing approvals and workflow complexity by using smart oversight controls

— Reducing the number of people involved in a transaction

— Proactively generating insights

— Improving relationships with fact-based information

— Reducing the burden forced upon suppliers

As Section II will explain, digital principles rely on free-flowing data with a singular golden supplier record. Once that data is available, procurement folks need to know what to do with it. In some cases, actions simply need to be automated. With digital procurement, it should be easy to onboard new clients or plug in new tools, suppliers, and requisitioners.

Digital procurement is not about *dashboards*, which are largely useless. Digital procurement is not about *mobile*, which is equally useless. If you're going to ask your technologists to send something to a mobile device, why not just automate it? Why do category managers need to sign off on $100,000 invoices *on their phones*? If it's a high-threshold capital purchase, it does need multiple sign-offs. But the problem isn't the device used for signing—it's that most organizations set those thresholds too low, creating meaningless approval tasks. When you move those tasks to mobile, guess what? They're still meaningless! This is not an effective use of technology and reinscribes procurement as a shadow budget control function rather than a value creator. We need to reframe this entire discussion around *signal-strategy-action*. What are the signals (changes in forecast, emerging disruptions, fluctuating stock)? How do these signals affect the strategy (do we stockpile, redistribute our supply allocation, pay more money)? What action(s) need to be taken, automated or otherwise (run an event, change lead times, notify customers)? The signal-strategy-action construct, as will be discussed in more depth in Sections 2.8 and 3.5.2, is a useful way I developed to understand how to apply machine-generated intelligence into day-to-day operations.

Furthermore, digital procurement is not about the variations of *artificial intelligence* (AI), *machine learning* (ML), or *robotic process automation* (RPA). Those are enablers. Procurement does not purchase AI, ML, or RPA—if it does, it's being taken for a ride. As a procurement professional, your vision is never "a blockchain"—your vision is a seamless and transparent supply chain with minimal administrative overhead. If someone can deliver that using blockchain technology, then good for them. But your vision is focused on results, not enablers. So, if someone is trying to sell you on the finer points of blockchain technology, it's like they're trying to sell you on the quality of rivets in the Brooklyn Bridge. The correct answer is not, *Oh, my gosh, I need to figure out how rivets work*. The correct answer is, *I'm happy to pay a reasonable toll to cross the East River, but I don't want to buy the Brooklyn Bridge*.

To take another example, RPA is fake automation. It's good for fixing broken business processes or a lack of systems integration. But in companies that have good business process planning and execution, and/or good systems integration, very little RPA exists. Real automation is the ability to take an action that a human is currently doing and teach a machine to do it instead. For example, *parametric bidding* (also known as *expressive bidding*) is hard to do. The bid sheets alone—usually complex Excel files—are unwieldy. Feeding bid sheets into optimization solvers, and interpreting the results, are no easy feats either. For that reason, many companies build centralized centers of excellence (CoEs) to serve as a clearing house for these types of activities. (By the way, this is considered a best practice.) But what if you could train a machine to run an expressive bidding event? In fact, this type of complex activity is uniquely suited to automation. Once you train the machine, you eliminate artificial limits to the number of events that you can run. This then increases your organization's ability to raise its event volume—and ideally its yields. A corresponding benefit is that the CoE resources can then be deployed elsewhere.

This discussion begs the question: do we need new playbooks? The short answer is yes. Nearly every playbook that exists was developed for an older generation of procurement objectives and people. You don't need to throw everything out—some fundamentals are still relevant. But you should be critical, even skeptical, when you are handed a "best practice playbook." The world has changed dramatically and most playbooks have not caught up. Some are simply too complex. Others fail to account for streamlined processes, new technology, or new ways of operating—including those prompted by COVID-19. By the way, simply adding the words "risk" or "sustainability" to existing playbooks isn't enough. For example, updating a playbook to, say, *identify sustainable suppliers to invite to an event* may look good on paper. But in light of all the technology disruption, that step is irrelevant and useless. So, we must be very critical of the idea of a digital best practice, because there aren't enough companies operating in the new digital environment, and the ones that do are engaging in a fair amount of experimentation. We don't yet have a statistically relevant number to be able to conclusively say what is a best practice.

The same is true for key performance indicators (KPIs) that measure what successful procurement looks like. Again, you need not completely toss out what you have. But you do need to acknowledge that generic benchmarks and platitudes that proclaim you a leader aren't good enough. If our goal is to deliver today's value with just 30 percent of today's resources, then we need new ways to measure our value contribution.

A view of the future

As we look to the future, procurement functions need to set aggressive efficiency targets. Otherwise, we are simply marching to obsolescence. We need to push our collective industry to create the same value as we do today— with just 30 percent of the resources. The only way to do this is to employ smart technology that allows us to automate procurement's mundane tasks.

We need to stop managing purchase orders (POs), doing approvals, looking for suppliers, consolidating performance data in Excel, or even running sourcing events. Fancy new technology can delight procurement employees, helping them to do their jobs quickly and efficiently while creating value—without the employees even realizing that the technology is saving the enterprise money.

Additionally, we in procurement should be using our control over corporate spend to accelerate and even expand ESG goals. The only way to achieve these goals is to put your money where your mouth is. Rather than merely praising diverse and/or green suppliers, we need to actually hire them; rather than merely talking about the value of diverse workforces, we need to ensure that our tier 1, 2, 3, n... suppliers have them; rather than merely condemning modern slavery, we need to prevent indirectly supporting it in our supply base.

As 3D printing, hyper-local manufacturing, and other digital trends take hold, business models are changing dramatically. This is going to open new opportunities for innovative growth. For example, imagine that you're a provider of traditional four-walls warehouse space. In today's market, you'll experience meaningful but finite growth. However, you could choose to move up the value chain to offer your customers more-automated warehouses featuring plenty of robots, 5G wireless connectivity, high ceilings, numerous in-town locations for better forward deployment of inventory, security services, and technology including a robust warehouse management system (WMS) and warehouse execution system (WES). If you do so, your growth potential in today's market is virtually unlimited. Who runs the effort to find, manage, and orchestrate new suppliers in support of all these innovative offerings, which will vary dramatically by geography? When a warehouse was just four walls, the procurement function was a low-value afterthought. Now it's finding and managing all these suppliers—and the suppliers' performance has a much bigger effect on the performance of the warehousing enterprise. Procurement has moved into a much more value-added position.

Given procurement's role in this new venture, why shouldn't the CPO take a top-line growth target? Where procurement innovates for margin improvement, why shouldn't we get revenue credit for that? The more we can become revenue generators rather than cost centers, the more we can open up greater streams of investment. Yet all these revenue-generating developments are driven by or enabled through digital advances. There has never been a better time to embrace digital, because there has never been a greater need for its transformative power.

Sadly, however, procurement is often still stuck in the 1990s. Digital tools are like a brand new car that we could drive from Los Angeles to Las Vegas, but if we entrust this car to people with traditional procurement mindsets, somewhere in the Mojave Desert they'll willfully drive the car into the ditch, smash the front end, deploy the airbags, step out, pour gasoline all over the mess, and drop a match on it. Then they'll pull out their phone to call a high-priced consultant and ask how to complete their trip. With the tools in this book—and a new digital-first procurement mindset—you'll be able to avoid that disaster. You'll take your new car to Vegas and win big.

Section I
How we got here

1.1 The woeful state of technology: the failures

Procurement technology is an abject failure. I cannot emphasize this enough. All we have to show for two decades of development and billions of dollars invested is overpromised benefits and under-delivered capabilities.

I know because I've been called in to help clean up the catastrophes. You don't hire Kearney to do a basic source-to-pay (S2P) systems implementation. You hire us either to solve a very complicated problem or to right things that have gone disastrously wrong. Many times in the past few years, I've received calls that weren't a proactive "Hey, here's an interesting, complicated problem," but a reactive "How can you save us?" This has given me a unique view into what works, what doesn't work, and the implications of overcommitting. I've distilled the main problem down to S2P benefits inflation, which vendors, analysts, and consultants are guilty of perpetuating. The benefits are built on patently faulty logic: increased sourcing, more robust compliance, process improvement. Increased sourcing savings activity is good, but hardly a prerequisite for a multimillion-dollar S2P implementation. The latter two benefits offer no clear measurable outcomes; they're simply stated benefit objectives. For example, if a benefit is stated as reduced cost of legacy technology, that assumes that someone is tracking existing expenditures and closing the loop to not only actually shut those tools down, but also to then remove that money from the budget. Otherwise, the cost *savings* are simply *cost redistribution*. Similarly, another key *benefit* promised in these business cases is process efficiency (more purchases on contract, fewer invoice exceptions, streamlined PO management), but how do we measure that impact? The true measure of this success would be to reduce the number of people supporting that work. Unfortunately, this outcome is rarely achieved and often any process efficiency gains are simply redirected to other low-value transactional activities. Suffice to say, this has created a massive trust gap.

A quick history

Procurement technology has evolved in several major phases (see figure 1). While the following brief summation massively simplifies complex cause-and-effect dynamics, it does illustrate the rough contours of how procurement technology lost its way.

First phase. In the late 1990s, under luminary leaders such as Tom Slaight and Pierre Mitchell, procurement software started to recognize the power of applying technology to traditional strategic sourcing. Amid the dotcom frenzy, a host of start-ups entered the scene. Their tools were rapid to deploy and relatively easy to use. They offered tangible benefits. Thus they established and, in some ways, formalized procurement operations.

Coupa, founded in 2006, sought to bring order to the chaos of requisitioning and payments. Building off that momentum, consultants started to frame the bigger picture of the linear S2P process. They created operating models of this process, which encouraged vendors to build to it. A host of end-to-end suite solutions emerged.

Second phase. In the early 2010s, suite providers started gobbling up the point solutions. For example, SAP bought Ariba and IBM bought Emptoris. Coupa, Concentra, and Jaggaer made their own acquisitions. By 2014 it looked like S2P procurement technology was solved.

Unfortunately, very little had actually been solved. All this consolidation depended on the naive assumption that in a closed-loop solution, information will flow seamlessly from module to module. Then the consolidators found out that running an end-to-end process is infinitely more complex than they had imagined—especially as acquisitions and divestitures became ever more common business practices.

Figure 1
Evolution of procurement timeline

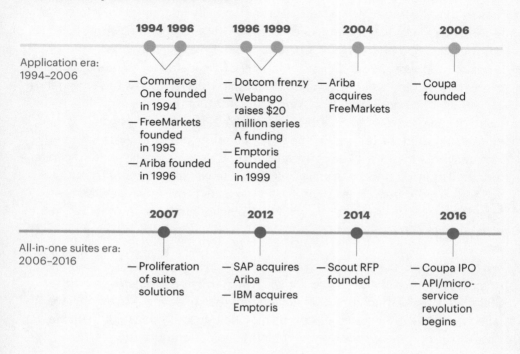

Application era: 1994–2006

1994 1996
— Commerce One founded in 1994
— FreeMarkets founded in 1995
— Ariba founded in 1996

1996 1999
— Dotcom frenzy
— Webango raises $20 million series A funding
— Emptoris founded in 1999

2004
— Ariba acquires FreeMarkets

2006
— Coupa founded

All-in-one suites era: 2006–2016

2007
— Proliferation of suite solutions

2012
— SAP acquires Ariba
— IBM acquires Emptoris

2014
— Scout RFP founded

2016
— Coupa IPO
— API/micro-service revolution begins

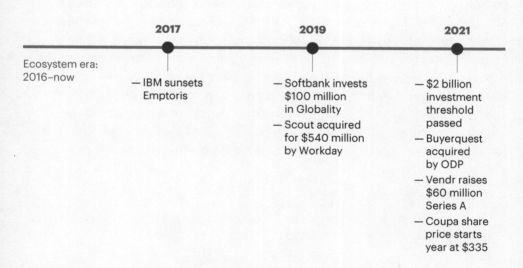

Ecosystem era: 2016–now

2017
— IBM sunsets Emptoris

2019
— Softbank invests $100 million in Globality
— Scout acquired for $540 million by Workday

2021
— $2 billion investment threshold passed
— Buyerquest acquired by ODP
— Vendr raises $60 million Series A
— Coupa share price starts year at $335

Source: Kearney and Digital Procurement World analysis

Third phase. Two trends, little understood at the time, doomed the technology. First, companies were finally realizing the technology itself was the only reason that the expected benefits weren't actually materializing. When the technology was still maturing, each company feared that its own people or processes had been at fault, but it turned out that everyone had the same types of problems. Second, new and vastly complicated innovations such as expressive bidding were flying under the radar. Thus, 2016 saw the emergence of new start-ups dedicated to solving problems that the suite providers had failed to solve, or even to remotely address. Available funding exploded, and entrants flooded the market. At the time of writing, procurement technology features more than 1,000 start-ups and more than $2 billion in venture capital funding.[1] Individually, these start-ups may take varying trajectories—but collectively, the trend is impactful. Had the suite providers delivered their promised value, these start-ups would have never emerged, at least not in the numbers we currently see.

Why aren't these start-ups being acquired as easily as before? Because the rationale for the suite no longer applies. The fully integrated closed-loop S2P system looks much better in PowerPoint than in action. Providers have failed to deliver, for extensive reasons that include lousy consultant advice, misaligned priorities, poor oversight, and needless complexity.

Meanwhile, broader technology trends may render the suite obsolete. Since 2016, the high-tech industry has centered around the microservices architecture approach and application programming interfaces (APIs). These twin revolutions have made everything inherently open and integrable. A popular example is the iOS or Android ecosystem: your phone doesn't need to be an end-to-end solution because it can serve as a platform for the apps you need. A more relevant example for procurement comes at the other end of the enterprise: Salesforce.com provides some level of core base functionality but gains its real power by sustaining a massive ecosystem of platform extensions.

---

[1] According to Kearney tracking of the top 100 start-ups funding amounts found on Crunchbase

Smart technology providers—led by Salesforce, Apple, Google, and Amazon—have thus built their products around this open exchange of data with their partners. Integration is seamless, and more importantly does not cost the customer extra. This new paradigm exposes the intellectual dishonesty of selling a customer a software license and then charging an additional fee to integrate third-party tools that improve on the provided functionality. Too many S2P providers have yet to catch on to this trend.

Where we are today

In 2020, there were six enterprise-level suites. I affably term them the Big Six: Coupa, iValua, Jaggaer, Oracle, SAP/Ariba, and Zycus (see figure 2 on page 22). As the figure shows, traditional S2P evaluation criteria show very little differentiation among them. Some providers spike in certain areas, others in different areas. There's no end-to-end winner. There's lots of mediocrity.

As the Big Six are challenged by well-capitalized start-ups, it's important to note that they can't simply buy their way out of their difficulties. The Big Six can expect declining revenues as customers lose interest in their big-bang approach to software. Additionally, as efficiency reduces the number of procurement employees using their software, the flaws in their licensing models will be exposed. Finally, only two of the Big Six (SAP and Oracle) have the cash to attempt such acquisitions—and they may not have the appetite. The start-ups have huge market valuations: in late 2019, Workday bought Scout for $540 million. Chasing start-ups at these prices is a bit like whack-a-mole, because as long as new opportunities exist to create value, start-ups will continue to enter the market. And unless the Big Six change the suite-solution nature of their approach to S2P software, those new opportunities will continue to exist.

Given these developments, it's appalling how many industry groups, consultants, and procurement groups evaluate vendors based on out-of-date evaluation frameworks. It's asinine to send a 300-question request for proposals (RFP) that asks for details on whether a vendor has a particular feature. This is a check-the-box exercise rather than a meaningful indicator of future success. Plotting and evaluating vendors on a 2x2 matrix is one dimension short of useful. Every enterprise's environment, strategies, and operating constraints are different.

Figure 2
The Big Six evaluation

Illustrative

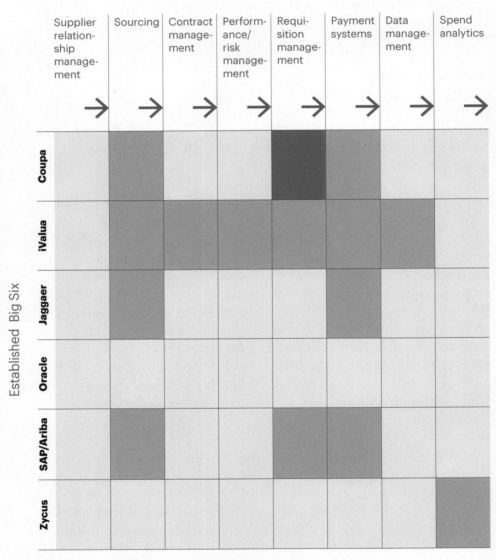

Source: Kearney analysis

For those in the back row who may not have heard that clearly, **depending on a generic vendor evaluation that is disconnected from your company's specific situation is destined for failure.** And by "specific situation," I don't simply mean "industry." For example, even within the medical industry, the operations of a healthcare provider such as a hospital system differ vastly from those of a medical device or pharmaceutical manufacturer. Good digital procurement practitioners (or consultants) should be able to evaluate a vendor's ability to deliver to the unique client situation rather than relying on generic third-party research. Ideally, clients should be able to make these evaluations without the need for either consultants or industry analysts. The problem is that while we all wait around for the industry pundits to evolve, the vendors are painting themselves into a box.

Today's industry groups and analysts are stuck in an old paradigm of evaluating accumulations of trivia. They're like bad high-school history teachers, who tested you on the rote memorization of names and dates. Smartphones and Wikipedia can tell us that the American Civil War started in 1861; what makes history come alive is understanding connections between, say, the Constitution, the Civil War, and the Black Lives Matter movement. Likewise, a procurement software tool is useful not for its internalized hundreds of pointless features but for when it helps you solve 2021's business problems. The evaluation shouldn't tell you that Tool A has only 234 features compared to Tool B's 400. Instead, it should tell you whether any of those features is the right one to meet your objective. A tool with the single right feature is far more valuable than one with 299 useless features. In procurement, we haven't switched to meet the reality of today's business environment.

Or at least we hadn't until the pandemic hit.

1.2 The completely wrong process

For more than two decades we in the procurement profession have labored under the traditional *upstream/downstream* process (see figure 3). This process looks great on paper: a linearly organized, compartmentalized, orderly way of conducting business. Unfortunately, it's also totally disconnected from the reality of what procurement needs to do—and, more importantly, what procurement *should* do.

This gets us back to an existential question: *why does procurement exist?* If procurement is intended to be a shadow budget organization that controls spend, then this process works. But if procurement wants to *add value*, to move beyond being the heel of the organization, then we need a completely different way of conceptualizing how procurement should operate. In fact, making such a transformation is less an *if* than a *must*. Budget controls to achieve annual cost savings will become increasingly automated. Procurement must add value—this change is inevitable.

Figure 3
Traditional procurement upstream/downstream process

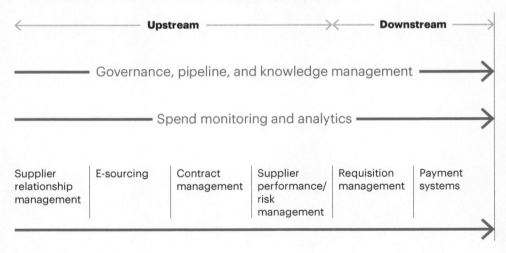

Source: Kearney analysis

Procurement has responsibility for the following fundamentals: analyze the market, source suppliers, contract with those suppliers, facilitate the requisitioning of the contracts, and ensure payment for goods and services delivered. What happens when we digitize and automate all these activities? It should free the next-generation procurement function to have a broader scope and address more complex business problems.

But before we can get there, we need to accomplish the automation, and/or make those traditional procurement functions self-service to the rest of the enterprise. While procurement must address the fundamentals, we need to stop focusing on low-value activities.

Suppliers and markets

From approximately 2008 to 2016, the Ariba Supplier Network (ASN) reigned supreme in the source-to-contract (S2C) landscape. Its value proposition was simple: Ariba hosted a network full of several million prequalified and onboarded suppliers that were integrated into the Ariba suite. If you became an Ariba customer, you could pay to have access to the network. If you used Ariba's procure-to-pay (P2P) software, you didn't have to worry about gathering and maintaining all the supplier information; you could requisition and pay a supplier without much management headache.

For some Ariba customers this worked in practice as well as it did in theory. But for most, it didn't. The problem was twofold. First, Ariba charged the supplier to onboard onto the network. (Although it provided a free option, that functionality was unusable.) This created a huge barrier to adoption by suppliers. Second, ASN shifted huge burdens onto suppliers. They had to fill out and maintain their information for every customer they served. In theory ASN was supposed to solve this, but for some reason it didn't. The charges and burdens placed on suppliers meant that some didn't sign up for ASN. Yet ASN assured procurement folks that it was the place they could go to find new suppliers. This promise failed to deliver. I know this because ASN-connected procurement people would continually hire us as consultants to help them find new suppliers.

Then other supplier networks came into the market. Now ASN is not the only game in town. In fact, it seems that nearly every solution has some sort of supplier network. Some vendors boast of having five million suppliers while others shout about having 20,000 *highly cultivated* suppliers. The proliferation of networks doesn't solve the problem of placing burdens on suppliers, but rather exacerbates it. Each vendor is trying to become the LinkedIn for suppliers, asking them to enter all their information into the network and maintain it on an ongoing basis, with that record made available to everyone who subscribes to the network. Imagine maintaining 20 different LinkedIn profiles!

A good supplier network creates value. It should be able to effectively onboard suppliers; house certifications and other compliance-related documentation; harmonize supplier entities; parent each supplier; and enrich data with sustainability, risk, and ESG information. It should be able to syndicate this information to any S2P platform, analytics tool, or productivity tool. But until such a solution emerges as the winner in this space, suppliers will remain stuck with this undue burden (see sidebar: Active supplier management).

1.3 The complicity of analysts, consultants, and industry groups

The procurement function has failed to achieve necessary maturity because analysts, consultants, and industry have a vested interest in perpetuating the status quo. These entities do provide useful services. They are not intentionally holding us back. But it's time to hold them to account.

The first problem is that they rely too heavily on *maturity models*. In particular, consultants will assess an organization's procurement capabilities with a plot of all the industry players. To make the plot work, there must be *leaders* and *laggards*, with everyone else distributed in between. But consultants are reluctant to acknowledge that these categories are arbitrary and that the entire distribution is skewed so that no company can achieve success. If you attained excellence, no more work would be required. So consultants arbitrarily extend the bar further and further. What's more, the criteria are highly subjective and non-scientific, even when the consultants layer in pseudo-scientific terms to give the illusion of legitimacy.

Active supplier management

Supplier experience is a major blind spot for *all* procurement systems and the people who buy them. If they paid attention, they might notice that 99 percent of the time that experience is awful. The systems create a lot of needless overhead, which the suppliers have to pass on to the customer in some way. Consider the supplier experience:

1 I am invited to sourcing events, often via tools that are complex and kludgy, and do not represent my interests.

2 If I'm successfully awarded the business, I'm then onboarded in a system where I have to enter all the contact and payment information in a process that is a few steps short of torture.

3 In parallel, I'm required to work with a customer's legal department on the contract. Usually it takes 30 emails and 20 revisions to a Word document before the contract is printed, signed, scanned, and emailed back.

4 Now I can provide my goods or service! But I have to do so with little or no feedback on performance except at quarterly business reviews.

5 Once a PO is generated, I submit my invoice and wait for payment. If any issues arise, the resolution process can be difficult and opaque. It may needlessly extend my payment timing for days, weeks, months (or many months).

6 I'm expected to keep my contact information and documentation up to date.

7 To cap all of this, I'm expected to respond to surveys at any given point about my risk posture and resilience capability. These surveys become the scourge of my productivity. To say that I have survey fatigue is a wild understatement. Every tool I work with is continually pinging me for the latest information on risk, ESG, sustainability, or contact information.

(continued on next page)

Active supplier management (continued)

There's no need for this. There is a better way. Good procurement processes can relieve the burden on suppliers. For example, a supplier chatbot could give suppliers greater visibility into chasing payment information. On the customer side, a bot could proactively watch payment terms and flag where a supplier should be paid but hasn't been.

Improved sourcing tools are easing the sourcing process for suppliers; over time the exchange concept (discussed in section 2.5.1) will further streamline overhead. The emergence of a winner in the supplier network will help the supplier information management (SIM) problem.

Note, however, that we also need to **stop the surveys.** They aren't as useful as we've been led to believe. How can they be, when suppliers are being inundated with them? The solution is twofold. First, we need to start employing active supplier relationship management (SRM). Most of the data we solicit from suppliers is publicly available and readily available from any number of data providers or by mining a supplier's activity across systems. This includes risk (event, financial, geography, cyber, and so on), sustainability, ESG, and certifications. The idea of uploading a certificate became outdated at about the same time as the flip cellphone. After all, let's be honest: nobody looks at a certificate once it's uploaded. It's often out of date and could even be blank. Instead, you should be automatically consuming certifications from the relevant certifying agency—that way you know you're up to date with the latest information.

In summary, good procurement processes use tools that relieve the burden on suppliers while improving the accuracy of information about them.

One day I was giving a briefing to the CPO of a CPG company. Year in and year out, this company scored as a leader in procurement excellence—in fact, *the* leader. So I said to the CPO, "I assume you have all your contracts in a single repository." From my perspective, this was the lowest possible bar to hit in contract life-cycle management (CLM). But he stopped me and asked why I would assume that. He said they had zero visibility into their contracts. We discussed the importance of basic contract visibility and we never managed to get to the broader briefing because it was clear they were nowhere near mature enough for that discussion. But his comment got me thinking: how can we describe a company as a leader in procurement when it lacks even basic visibility into its contracts? The answer: only by arbitrarily defining *maturity*.

Assessment instruments do have value. A company can gain insights from plots showing its maturity across various dimensions—it can more easily identify what needs to be fixed. Indeed, in a different meeting, one CPO walked to his filing cabinet and pulled out a well-worn copy of his Kearney Assessment of Excellence in Procurement (AEP) report and proceeded to point out all the areas of progress he and his team were making against the maturity benchmarks.

For digital procurement, assessments have particular value in identifying the improvement opportunities around organizational capabilities. Digital assessments should focus on the maturity of specific capabilities. More broad use of *leader/laggard* language is pejorative and does not reflect the reality of complex operating environments. For example, how do you evaluate a company that makes continual acquisitions? It ends up with dozens of enterprise resource planning (ERP) systems—I've seen as many as 180. These duplicated systems create a vast web of complexity, causing the company to struggle with data management. How does this company compare to one that does no acquisitions, has a single ERP system, and struggles to manage its services spend? Answer: you shouldn't compare them, because the point of an assessment tool should not be to label a company as an overall *leader* or *laggard*. Unfortunately, simply having a particular tool doesn't mean that you'll make good use of it. Instead, digital procurement assessments should focus on existing capabilities (inclusive of pain points) balanced against corporate objectives (investment levels, risk tolerance, ESG goals, and so on) and desired maturity level (not every company wants or needs to excel in every competency).

Meanwhile, there's an incestuous web among vendors, industry analysts, and industry groups. Vendors pay to be assessed by industry analysts. But industry analysts have no incentive to change their evaluation models. They send the vendors massively complex RFPs which, despite being onerous, contain little insight. What's the point of asking a sourcing provider if it has ten auction styles or one hundred? This is the perfect example of technology for technology's sake—the point of technology should be to solve a business problem. Why does it matter how many auction styles a tool has? All that matters is whether the tool has the auction style that your business needs, the style that aligns with your procurement group's objectives. Simply stated, industry analysts perform their evaluations without any context of strategy or real-world environment.

Moreover, once a tool is implemented in the real world, there's not much of a feedback loop to indicate how it's performing. For example, one S2P provider has long scored high on the industry analysts' 2x2 evaluations—the analyses that evaluate vendors on two dimensions (such as cost and maturity, or cost and adoption, or adoption and future vision) and plot each vendor in relation to the others. The high scores are surprising, given considerable real-world evidence suggesting massive overstatement of that S2P's capabilities and an inability to deliver. These 2x2s also lack real-world input on company performance. Is it struggling financially? Is it losing talent? Is it losing deals left and right and, if so, why? The 2x2s also try to put everything into neat little boxes, thus struggling with components that don't fit or account for new categories of innovation. For example, what if my company needs to calculate rebates into our financial modeling? Or what if we plan to resell procurement services? It could be something that's highly valuable to a procurement organization in a particular industry, but if it doesn't fit the analysts' all-industry model, it doesn't get evaluated. Finally, these analyses offer little or no accounting for broader macro changes or disruptions in procurement operations models. Procurement—especially good digital procurement—depends on factors much broader than whether a tool employs AI or has a mobile interface. How can the tool enable a change in approach to governance? How can it help us review the type of people we should be hiring? No 2x2 evaluation or industry analyst report will ever illustrate that level of complexity or nuance.

The problem with industry groups is they charge membership fees to their members. Then they charge vendors to participate. In return, the vendors get members' contact information. It's an odd, outdated revenue model: contact information is not exactly a scarce resource. It's almost always available from a free, easy-to-use tool that most people are familiar with, called Google. So exactly what function do industry groups serve? The typical answer is *certifications, learning, networking,* and *conferences.* Again, it's a decades-old business model that doesn't reflect today's reality. First, getting more certifications rarely turns out to lead to increased monetary compensation.[2] Second, what you can learn at a conference—though sometimes worthwhile—depends on the speakers. When a conference's vendors or sponsors speak, or if it's pay-to-speak, the content is subpar at best. Plenty of speakers go from conference to conference, regurgitating the same content, which might be years or even decades old. Third, networking at in-person conferences suffers from the terrible job that big conferences do at creating accessible moments. You can often get some networking done at smaller conferences, but in the era of LinkedIn, you can network dynamically and continually online. So, while the in-person conference provides some value (and a trip to a lovely destination), its return on investment was elusive and probably diminishing even pre-COVID-19. After the crisis, it's hard to imagine that all these in-person conferences will remain as relevant.

The most damaging parties are consultants who are also vendor resellers. They mask their bias by pointing to the industry analyst reports. This circular logic shows exactly why their services are a disservice. And by the way, the solution to this dilemma doesn't have to be *hire unbiased consultants.* If you want to hire me, I'm happy to take your money. But the best answer is for each organization to have people with the skills to make their own assessments and market evaluations. If you want to be a top-notch digital procurement organization, you need to be continually monitoring, evaluating, and testing solutions in the market. Once you have those skills, industry analysts and consultants become irrelevant (see sidebar on page 32: The folly of depending on 2x2 evaluations).

[2] Procurement Foundry's annual salary compensation salary study, https://procurementfoundry.slack.com/files/UHCPADSRL/F01LMB30MTJ/ 2020_salary_and_comp_survey_final.pdf

The folly of depending on 2x2 evaluations

A few years ago, I connected with the founder of a technology company. He had built a small S2P system and wanted to expand into new markets. I let him pitch to me for 45 uninterrupted minutes. When he was done, I gave him the bad news: in the market he wanted to enter, everything he had built (end-to-end visibility, centralized purchasing, Amazon-like interfaces, supplier golden records) was already commoditized, or was about to be commoditized.

He was shocked and disappointed. He couldn't believe it. He kept saying that he had read all the analyst reports, which allowed him to extrapolate (guess) the gaps in the market. It hadn't occurred to him that the analysts were neither accurately reporting on the start-up disruptions in the market nor contextualizing the broader change in business operations. You could say that he didn't do his due diligence—but he apparently thought that reading industry analyst reports *was* due diligence.

While this is an extreme example, it's sadly not the only one: I have talked to several clients where what the 2x2 showed differed diametrically from what was delivered.

1.4 Conclusion

As you can see there is no shortage of villains and challenges. Again, the goal here is to acknowledge where we have collectively not hit the mark. This is a situation of our own making (which includes me), but it is also one in which we can both reverse and simultaneously create a new more exciting tomorrow. To effect this change, we will need to fundamentally reimagine procurement around a strong digital competency. The next section will get into exactly how we do that.

Section II
The path to digital

2.1 What to do

The previous section identified the problem procurement faces today: a colossal lack of digital maturity, increased macro disruptions, and an entrenched legacy of mediocre performance. In this section we'll examine what to do about it: how to build a digital strategy, what technological advancements to expect, and why the future will be different. But first let's acknowledge that you have to do *something*.

Are you truly leading your procurement organization toward digital enablement? Or are you allowing what might have been reasonable excuses in the past to block your progress? The first step toward leading change is to stop rationalizing why digital transformation isn't possible in your organization. Digital procurement technology has evolved, the expectations for leadership regarding digital technology has changed, and the opportunity has arrived for those who are able to seize it.

2.2 Stop making excuses

If the mantra of the Zoom-infested COVID-19 era is the reminder, "You're on mute," the mantra of the past 20 years of procurement mediocrity is, "We're an SAP shop so we chose Ariba." Simply saying, "We're an SAP shop" is not a strategy. It's an excuse. It's an abdication of responsibility, a resigned acquiescence that IT must know best. There are many things IT knows best about: servers, networks, laptops, and so forth. IT people do not know best about the procurement business—nor should they be expected to; that's not their job. And yet I hear, "We're an SAP shop" at least five times a week. Shockingly, I hear it amid postmortems on failed Ariba implementations where the failure has already occurred and millions of dollars have already been wasted.[1] It's as if an organizational paralysis has set in, and everybody's waiting for a wizard to wave a magic wand that will make everything better. There is no wizard. Things are not going to get better by simply pleading with SAP (or Oracle), because your failure is not their fault. They didn't run the evaluation, make the choice, or write the check.

Another phrase I hear a lot is, "Our IT group won't allow it." That's an equally poor excuse for inaction. IT organizations have no issue with Salesforce as the commercial platform for sales and marketing. Once Salesforce is implemented, IT organizations take a back seat and let the business experts do what they need to do on that platform. Why shouldn't procurement and the supply chain work in the same way? Nearly every procurement activity generates a tremendous return, traditionally in cost savings and efficiencies, but also increasingly in support of top-line growth. Why do we procurement people have such a low opinion of ourselves that in a conversation with IT we'd act as if we didn't deserve to get what we need? Moreover, when it comes to procurement technology, we are the stakeholder. It is our choice to pick what works for us, not what works for others. Often we spend so much time helping others make decisions that perhaps we forget what it's like to be the one whose needs must be met. Never pass up the chance to employ the authority that being the stakeholder confers, otherwise you have nobody to blame but yourself.

Limiting your vision because of prior technology choices or deferring responsibility to the IT department are traps to avoid. Digital transformation strategy is set by business leaders and supported by IT. Take a minute and ask yourself whether you've fallen into this trap. If so, you aren't alone. What's important is what you do now. Will you push the excuses to the side and lead your procurement organization? Will you step forward and drive the formation of digital enablement strategy?

---

[1] There is nothing empirically wrong about choosing SAP, or any provider for that matter, if procurement makes a deliberate strategic choice. Also, this is not to single out SAP Procurement/Ariba over the other S2P providers; there have been many millions of dollars wasted on all the providers.

2.3 Set the strategy

Those that seek to build an advantaged procurement organization with digital technology will need to first build broad alignment to a digital transformation strategy. The alternative approach of running pilots and generally monitoring the space might sound attractive because it allows procurement leaders to say they're addressing the digital procurement opportunity. However, taking small steps without alignment will almost certainly result in zero change. If you aspire to leading your organization and driving change, you must have an aligned strategy.

The reason an aligned strategy is important is because there are many choices for the digital enablement of procurement, and these choices affect colleagues in your organization. You will need these colleagues to help effect the change. If they haven't had input or if they don't agree, they'll likely oppose your efforts.

The important choices that need to be addressed in your digital enablement strategy include:

— What is the value that will be delivered by implementing the digital strategy? Does the pursuit of this value align with business priorities?

— Which technologies and capabilities are needed to deliver the value?

— How will we change the work that we do (as opposed to simply automating what we do today)?

— How will we change how we work (agile and responsive as opposed to fixed processes)?

— What roles will be required in the new model? What capabilities will be needed to fill these roles?

— How aggressively should we drive change?

Can you imagine the differing views on the important questions above? Of course. This is why it's important to create the opportunity to address the hard questions before positions get solidified. The starting point is to clearly articulate the specific pain points to be addressed and the value that will be delivered through this success. Once you have identified the value to pursue, the choices of technology, process, roles, capabilities, and speed of change are all important. Choosing a path forward requires evaluating the trade-offs that will optimize impact, cost, and speed while offsetting risk.

All these decisions will have implications on existing process, people, and organizational elements. This will force the assessment of what needs to be altered, bolstered, or excised. More specifically, within procurement do we have the skills and capabilities required to take the digital journey and, if not, how do we fill the gaps? Finally, we need to determine the organizational readiness and tolerance to undertake this journey. Hand in hand with the readiness requirement is whether we have the leaders in the business and of course the executive sponsorship to champion the journey.

Avoiding the work to ensure alignment and direction typically results in wasted time and effort. We recommend that companies set strategy through a four-step process:

— Evaluate the opportunity

— Identify potential solutions

— Build the future state aspiration

— Make the case for change

As the bullets show, the procurement organization needs to focus on strategy and mission to make procurement functions self-service, intelligent, and empower forward-looking decision-making. This simple diagram visualizes the correlation between digital competency and ability to deliver value to the business. More importantly, no matter where a company is in its journey, it can see a path to the future.

2.3.1 Evaluate the opportunity

The purpose of this step is to build a realistic baseline assessment of the current procurement technology and identify potential opportunities to effect value. Determining an organization's procurement technology maturity is a relatively straightforward exercise (see figure 4 on page 38). This figure provides a rough gauge of digital procurement maturity. First, we want to know whether there's a strategy for procurement technology, data, and analytics. Sometimes these enterprises have recently gone through (or are currently going through) a digital transformation, which is good, but all too often they're surface level when they get to procurement. Next, we need to figure out how much we're spending on procurement technology. Often this exercise will ferret out unnecessary complexity and expenditures. It will also identify areas where service providers are being used (where market tools should be employed). Then we understand how the system is used, identify pain points, process inefficiencies, and evaluate general user experience (UX). Additionally, we need to ask our users what they think. This is almost always a painful exercise because most procurement groups are set up to slow users down rather than enable them so there's a natural bias toward negative feedback. Finally, what organizational capabilities are we lacking, either in procurement or in the organization more broadly? The result of this work should be clarity on the pain points, key stakeholders who have provided input and felt heard, and alignment on potential opportunities to address (see sidebar on page 39: Process analytics tools).

2.3.2 Identification

The identification of potential solutions involves matching today's procurement technologies with the pain points and business opportunities pinpointed in the previous step. This requires having a baseline understanding of the scores—really hundreds—of digital procurement solutions that are available. It's important to triage the universe of solutions to those that have sufficient maturity and provide a business and technology fit with your organization.

Successful procurement organizations will curate a set of prospective technology providers and have a series of meetings to identify the specific use cases. Conducting these meetings within a few days allows for the further triage and identification of potential solutions to take forward. This triage

Figure 4
Stages of digital procurement maturity

Future-looking	Procurement services delivered to the user	Extensible micro services-based architecture	Best-of-breed plug-and-play apps	Proactive insight generation and actions	Fully automated and digitized business processes
Working toward the future	Digital team architecting and exploring new tech	Function-specific niche solutions (non-integrated)	Central data hub with single source of truth	Pilot AI/ML-based technologies	
Meeting the minimum	Disconnected procurement systems	Dedicated analytics team to build insights	RPA to automate processes		
Impaired	Multiple data sources	Ad hoc offline analytics and BI	Manual/offline processes		

Source: Kearney analysis

Process analytics tools

Process analytics tools look at how users operate a system or a collection of systems by analyzing transactional logs. This is a fact-based, bottom-up examination of existing processes. It surfaces how users are navigating and engaging with systems. This can dramatically speed up the baseline process mapping and identify process-efficiency opportunities. Process analytics tools are a fundamental piece of a digital foundation. If you don't have such a tool in place already, check with your IT group as they may be using this for other functions, and if not, this is an opportunity to partner with them.

is characterized by an assessment of solution maturity and fit with identified business needs and opportunities. The conclusion of this work is typically excitement and enthusiasm for the potential solutions to the identified pain points and opportunities. These are the building blocks for a future state that will enable the procurement organization to be a better business partner and to drive more value. It's important to involve the important stakeholders in the organization with this process as they will better understand the possibilities and will become proponents of building the new capabilities.

2.3.3 Future state aspiration

The future state aspiration should be guided by stakeholder preferences, current best practices, and required capabilities. There is a minimal core set of capabilities that needs to be achieved for any procurement organization. Beyond that there is a broad set of opportunities to pursue. It's important to choose the right opportunities and to pursue them effectively. This presupposes one has a future state aspiration that describes the opportunities, the potential solutions, and the value to be achieved.

Getting to the right set of opportunities can be challenging. For example, take contract life-cycle management (CLM). Best practices will tell you that you need: a contract repository, contract life-cycle management (workflows, established thresholds, and so on), e-signature, compliance, authoring (templates, contract clauses, and the like), and contract analytics and automation. On paper this looks great and many companies will buy a CLM tool that offers most of these features and start the implementation. First, they deploy a contract repository, which usually goes okay. Then they do a significant amount of hard work to define all the process permutations and program all the workflows. After six to nine months (or longer) laboring under this delusion, this is exactly when the money runs out as legal, procurement, and the unlucky business stakeholders assigned to this project churn through all the complexity without coming to a satisfactory conclusion. It's like a tie in football: nobody lost, but nobody won, which is really a loss given the money and resources expended. If they manage to work through this, next up is e-signature, which is straightforward. Then the wheels completely come off at contract authoring because this requires massive change management effort that procurement can't influence and legal rarely seeks to undertake. The worst part of this is that all these tasks are good to do—they're "best practices" after all—but none creates value for the business user. None of them reduces the SLAs for onboarding a new supplier. None of them tells category managers where risk sits in their contracts. None of them reduces contract clause complexity. The key lesson here is that the future state aspiration must be grounded in opportunities that will not only drive value for the business but also have the support of key stakeholders.

Why not start with the items that will create value for the business now? Put all the contracts into a logical repository. Then point contract analytics tools at the contracts. This will create amazing and immediate benefits for the business user. The best part is that this can be done in three to six weeks and for a fraction of the cost. Once this is done, slowly and deliberately the other CLM best practices can be undertaken. This should be repeated across the entire procurement value chain.

The result of this work should be a future state aspiration that's compelling to the business owners and to those that will need to do the work of managing the change. Practically speaking, this means that the work is built on an understanding of the business opportunities, a clear-eyed assessment of potential solutions, and a thoughtful prioritization of solutions and business value at stake. Addressing this properly will yield a clear picture of a much better future that will create significant value for the business (see figure 5).

Figure 5
Digital capabilities and phasing by functional area

Capabilities

Procurement enablement	Supplier management	Sourcing	Category management	Contracting	Requisition	Payment	Plan/make	Data and analytics	Risk management	Environmental, sustainability, governance
Pipeline/performance management	Segmentation	Basic sourcing	Templated category management	Contract repository	Marketplace	Accounts payable	Forecast demand	Spend visibility	Cyber	Sustainability ratings
Request intake	Crowd-sourcing	Sourcing optimization	Smart category management	Analytics and automation	Category solutions (multiple)	Invoice management	Commodity trading and risk management	Benchmarks/pricing	Financial	Diverse supplier identification
Process mining	Identification	Tail spend automation		E-signature		P-cards	CM visibility/collaboration	Market forecasts	Supply risk	Paper digitization
Robotic process automation	Performance	Tail of tail		Contract life-cycle management		Fraud detection and identity verification			Event	Carbon tracking
Scouting	Collaboration	Automated sourcing		Smart contracts		Dynamic discounting			Reputational	Regenerative farming
Dynamic road mapping	Relationship					Working capital optimization			N-tier visibility	Compliance and audit
Digital ledger technology	Transactional					Tax optimization			Regulatory	
						Cryptocurrency				

Legend: ● Short   ● Medium   ● Long

Platforms

API-centric infrastructure	Data foundation	Analytics	Risk

Source: Kearney analysis

The figure shows a sample breakout of those various aspects. It's formatted as a "heat map" to indicate initial phasing and prioritization based on maturity of capability. We've been discussing contracting, but you'll have a future state aspiration for each of the columns in the figure.

2.3.4 Building the case for change

The successful digital enablement of the procurement function requires strong support from key stakeholders in the organization. Procurement's internal business customers need to see enough benefit for them that they'll be willing to invest the time to learn new work processes. Finance will need to see a business case that is compelling relative to all the other potential investments they could make. Individuals within the procurement organization need to see a benefit for them personally to support the change. Building alignment is a requirement for driving change, but how this is best achieved varies by organization.

The most common mistake we see among those seeking to drive change in procurement is that they don't invest enough time helping key stakeholders in the organization see the opportunity they see. The building blocks of communication materials include clarity on the opportunity, why it is right for your company, and the value it will deliver. The fourth step of building the case for change addresses this directly by creating three primary outputs:

— Communication materials to describe the opportunity

— Rationale for why the technology, capabilities, and pace of change are the right solution

— Quantified business case showing ROI for investment

Winning the support of your colleagues will never be as simple as building the aforementioned outputs. It is crucial to understand the barriers to change, which decision-makers will sway the tide, and how to chart a path to alignment. Often this involves engaging your business stakeholders in setting direction or engaging with finance on a thoughtful investment approach. Regardless of what's needed in your organization, it requires work and attention. But achieving true alignment upfront will give you the support you need to then drive these valuable changes through the organization. Don't get caught in the trap of building the perfect answer in isolation. Spend your time winning the support of the people who matter.

2.4 A new architecture: the procurement ecosystem

For the past two decades, the procurement profession has labored under the delusion that the world is a flat, linear source-to-pay process. By now the failure of that vision has become clear. The central argument of this book is that procurement and the way business operate today have fundamentally changed. We desperately need a more flexible and extensible architecture to match the way we need to operate in a world of chaos.

In short, the procurement world is round and not flat. To succeed in this world, you need an ecosystem approach that's built on a solid data foundation, offers a plug-and-play choice of easily onboarded apps, gives users a delightful, burden-free experience, and features an intelligence layer that produces insights across the entirety of the operating system. Imagine having an iPad of apps that are tied to a central hub. All you have to do is pop open whichever app you want to use and start doing your work. You can run your sourcing event, make a requisition, or do market research—all from apps on this hub. Behind the scenes, they're seamlessly integrated to provide you with the data and functionality you require.

Procurement needs to get to a place where we no longer have to manipulate data in Excel—such tasks result from bad data and a lack of relevant system-generated insights. We should be able to dial up an automated service bot (such as Siri or Alexa) to requisition anything we need without having to cut and paste material to enter briefs into a tool. Those are tasks a bot should do for us.

2.4.1 The spider chart

A graphic representation of that procurement ecosystem is shown in figure 6 on page 44. I call it the spider chart. It is the central message of this book: various procurement functions can and should serve as apps integrated into a central hub. That hub (or exchange—call it what you will) consists of a user interface, integration layer, data foundation, and intelligence capabilities.

Figure 6
The spider chart

Illustrative

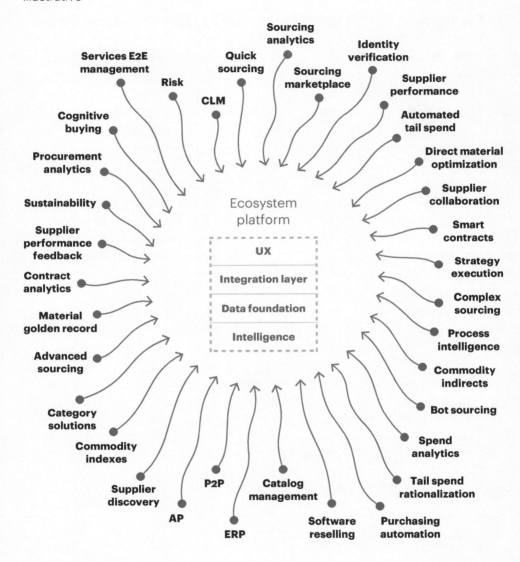

Source: Kearney analysis

At first glance, the figure may seem intimidating. Indeed, it's meant to be overwhelming, because we won't do procurement well until we wrap our heads around just how complex it can be. A lot of potential solutions circle this hub. Not every company will use every solution—you may only use five or six of them. But every procurement person should know that there's a bigger universe out there.

At the same time, however, the figure should not be intimidating, because it's just like your phone. Imagine trying to graphically map all the apps on your iPhone or Android device—and the way, for example, that your contacts database merges with your texting, emailing, or telephoning apps. This is the same principle. For that matter, if you have experience with Salesforce.com, imagine a graphic representation of its many apps. This is that same model applied to procurement.

Furthermore, the business user will never see or care about this complexity. You will purchase an ecosystem provider to organize the chaos, just as you paid Apple or Android to organize the chaos of your phone. And, as noted above, you'll prioritize a delightful user experience when you select the right ecosystem provider.

The figure may also appear complex because it shows so many individual capabilities. In the case of risk, for example, you may use just one of those providers today. But part of my goal for this book is to show how you can take advantage of the innovative accomplishments of today's many high-tech procurement start-ups to meet the procurement of tomorrow. What is on the chart is what we know today, but there are continually new solutions hitting the market that will further expand and deconstruct the procurement value chain. So the complexity is ever growing. To address this complexity procurement, people need to understand and stay on top of these trends. We can no longer rely solely on analysts and consultants to do this work for us.

The spider chart represents the procurement value chain deconstructed as we know it today. These capabilities can be easily mapped to existing solutions in the marketplace. For example, it's no longer good enough to have a single sourcing tool. Twenty years of mediocrity has taught us that we need at least five different sourcing tools. We need one for basic sourcing, one for tail spend (ideally automated), one for tail-of-the-tail, one for sourcing optimization, and one for complex categories. In figure 7, we see how these precise digital tools can be applied to the various spend pools. For risk, we need at least seven tools (event, cyber, macro, financial, reputational, geographic, supply), but that number will grow as we better understand the various threat vectors. For each functional need, there will be more and more precise solutions. Success will come from the precision in each functional area.

I often show the spider chart in presentations. It's very popular. It sparks tremendous discussion. Lots of companies reach out to me, wanting to be included on the chart. But I don't give participation trophies. Does your company do something specific and precise? The big opportunity here is the white space in and around what we know today. Many more solutions are coming to solve problems we haven't identified yet or problems that will arise as a result of the continual changes to our business operations. A good digital platform will enable all these solutions. A good process capability will enable the organization to flex and respond to changing conditions, whether external disruptions (natural disaster, pandemic, trade war, and so on) or internal changes (expansion, M&A, and the like). For example, the processes for dealing with trade wars differ greatly from those for dealing with a pandemic. Meanwhile, cost savings should be automatic. Requisitioning should be self-service and have built-in cost efficiencies.

2.4.2 The requirements for a procurement ecosystem

At the center of the spider chart is the hub. As shown in the spider chart, it has four key components, or requirements. Let's look at each in turn.

A delightful user experience

The spider chart is the procurement view of the world. But it's not what end users care about. Those users should be shielded against all its complexity. We need to bring procurement services to where the user is.

Figure 7
Approaching sourcing tools

| Strategically managed spend | Tail spend | Tail of the tail |

Spend by supplier

Sourcing tools and levers

Basic sourcing

— E-sourcing tool

Self-serve category-specific solutions

— IT
— Travel
— Legal
— Facilities management
— Print
— Professional services

Advanced sourcing with SMEs and automation

— Expressive bidding

Automation and catalogs

— No-touch sourcing on requisitions (three bids and a buy)

Automation and outsourcing

— Low-volume suppliers

Source: Kearney analysis

In our personal lives we're familiar with Amazon's easy-to-use, intelligent platform, which makes buying not only simple but also pleasurable. The entire Amazon experience is based on information transparency, giving the user qualified recommendations, but also full information transparency to facilitate trade-offs among cost, quality, warranty, delivery, and so on. Amazon also gives us the ability to see what "others like me" have purchased.

And yet, in the corporate procurement environment we've plateaued the thinking at providing portals and catalogs. That's technology that hasn't improved measurably from the 1990s. Cross-catalog search is still very much a work in progress and in practice users either have to click-and-click-and-click-and-click only to find what they're looking for is not in the catalog. Or worse, they search and can't find what they're looking for because there are thousands of irrelevant results or they are somehow not searching the proper catalog. This can have painful implications for suppliers.

Indeed, in many cases organizational and governance complexity have made corporate portals harder to use. For example, punchouts—a link to an external catalog hosted by a particular supplier—were a way to work around limitations of portal technology by extending the selection of products available for purchase without having to continually extend the portal itself. However, punchouts take users away from the core site, which is problematic as they almost always have different user experiences, and they make reporting and transactional reconciliation difficult.

Moreover, we're today moving away from traditional PCs and laptops into the iOS/Android era. Your apps need to as well. To be clear, I'm not saying that your technology should have a mobile interface—I'm saying that mobile is the endgame. PCs are deprecated with no central organizing principle, or at least an outdated one. With iOS or Android, you have a core UX, integration, and intelligence that underlies all apps. Plus you have an app store. These strengths mean that eventually all business operations will move to iOS/Android devices. Procurement systems should match this trend.

Does the app integrate natively with other apps, does it conform to good app design standards, and, most importantly, how does it interact with the core operating system to make use of platform-level intelligence? Intelligent bots should be able to procure what the user needs with the requisite oversight rather than a highly controlled, intensely governed approach.

A good user experience shouldn't be dependent on weeks or months of training. It should be intuitive. It should enable compliance without scare tactics. Rollout should be vastly simplified and benefits immediate. If I can't do my work on an interface as simple as an iPad, then we have used the wrong criteria to design and select our apps because the UX interface is needlessly complex and requires too much training. An overly complex UX is not sufficiently taking advantage of the system intelligence to guide users to the desired outcome. Instead it's putting the burden on the user to take the right action even if that action is not clear or doesn't exist. Moreover, apps that depend on extensive training almost always lead to poor adoption. Today's business user has an ever-growing set of responsibilities heaped onto their plate and having to take the time to learn, not to mention remember, how a tool works is not an effective use of that person's time. Nobody had to teach me how to use an iPhone—why would we make procurement more complex? At Amazon, technology sits in the background to guide and encourage me to buy more things that I didn't know I wanted—procurement should similarly leverage smart technology to create the outcomes we want.

The hub thus brings together everything I need to do my job. And it does so as slickly as the iPad brings together everything else in my life (see figure 8 on page 50).

Integration layer

If you spend $10 million on an S2P system, you shouldn't be charged an extra penny, much less $1 million, to integrate another solution. This is intellectually dishonest. The client shouldn't be responsible for paying for integrations, especially in 2021. Most of the start-ups that support the spider chart integrate with one another because integration is straightforward. If you're paying for integrations you are doing it wrong—integration is the responsibility of the vendors.

Figure 8
Bringing it all together

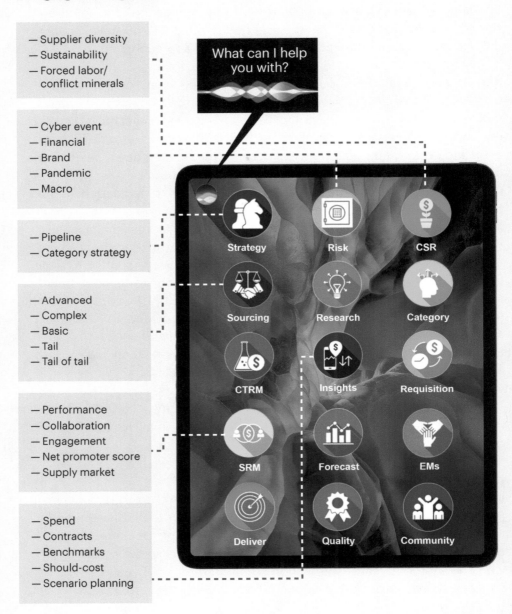

— Supplier diversity
— Sustainability
— Forced labor/
   conflict minerals

— Cyber event
— Financial
— Brand
— Pandemic
— Macro

— Pipeline
— Category strategy

— Advanced
— Complex
— Basic
— Tail
— Tail of tail

— Performance
— Collaboration
— Engagement
— Net promoter score
— Supply market

— Spend
— Contracts
— Benchmarks
— Should-cost
— Scenario planning

What can I help you with?

Strategy   Risk   CSR

Sourcing   Research   Category

CTRM   Insights   Requisition

SRM   Forecast   EMs

Deliver   Quality   Community

Source: Kearney analysis

Naturally, this means that any provider that wants to be the center hub not only needs to possess technical integration capability (most of the Big Six do) but also needs to facilitate its ecosystem in a way that makes start-up apps want to be part of it (very few do). The iPhone would never have survived without the explosion of apps that followed its release. In the process, the app developers benefited as well. Having an app in the Apple App Store is a badge of honor and a source of great benefit. The same has to be true for the hub provider.

This philosophy is antithetical to the flat-world thinking of the past. The Big Six treated everything as a zero-sum game, so they saw the ability to integrate with an external best-of-breed solution as taking value away rather than enhancing it. If you wanted to use someone else's contract management tool instead of a Big Six provider's default tool, you were taking money away from them. So they did everything they could do to dissuade you from taking that action. They boasted of their own built-in end-to-end integration, charged you premiums for external integrations, or simply bought up companies they perceived as a risk.

Thus, part of the challenge of this new ecosystem is finding a way whereby the hub and the point solution can mutually benefit. As noted in Section 2.4.4, two of the Big Six are making active strides toward this vision. For the rest, they're facing difficult long-term strategic decisions. Given the value of this market, there's no doubt that other new entrants will make a play for the middle over the next couple years.

Data foundation

If your goal is controlling spend, then your entire data foundation will be built on the primacy of every transaction. This is the epitome of *spend management*. This gives you absolute control over where the spend is going and who it's going to. It unlocks the ability to look at purchasing trends over time and compare purchases to benchmarks and a set of available suppliers. You do still harmonize supplier record, but only in service to the spend.

Spend management can be achieved. I have seen it. I have seen it succeed with all the existing vendors. I have seen it unlock benefits such as funneling spend to channels, spend visibility, and fraud detection. If that's your goal, then it can be done. The problems surface when you try to do anything strategic, including sourcing. It doesn't work.

However, if you're a mature organization and have sufficient control over your spend (through digital or operating-model controls) then controlling spend should be secondary to other components of value creation. For these purposes, your entire data foundation needs to be based on the *supplier golden record*. This is a single source of truth for every supplier—a record that is cleaned, harmonized/parented, classified, and enriched. The supplier golden record sets you up for value creation, top-line growth, advanced savings, partnership opportunities, sustainability, diversity, and innovation. Here you still have spend visibility, but the focus is on the supplier first. You want the ability to track performance, interactions, and capabilities, and you want to syndicate that knowledge into every transactional system. Typically, this syndication is an afterthought, but when we center on supplier golden records, it's the crucial thread that holds the entire digital fabric together.

You want the ability to ingest all transactions, contracts, supplier golden records, and external signaling. This is a conceptual framework, not a literal system. More importantly, we need the ability to ingest upstream data from planning systems and use that to collaborate with suppliers to tell them how much supply we need and when. We also need to be able to consume data from operational systems such as manufacturing, quality, transportation management, and warehouse management. All data doesn't have to physically reside here, but it needs to be syndicated in a way that can be easily accessible.

It's important to note that the data foundation is best delivered and managed by a third party versus in-house because they're going to be able to keep supplier records up to date in a way that's more useful than can be done by a procurement organization's individual supplier portal. In fact, the concept of every procurement organization having its own supplier portal is perhaps one of the great failures of procurement technology and it holds back our collective function.

The data foundation provides a single place for suppliers to go and manage their key data and attributes (see figure 9). The repository tracks all certifications, diversity, sustainability, banking, and other relevant information. The data foundation captures this information as suppliers upload their certificates. This construct has the advantage that every time a supplier is added, its website is automatically scraped for additional context, an activity that can be repeated automatically. Going further, a good data foundation

Figure 9
Data foundation

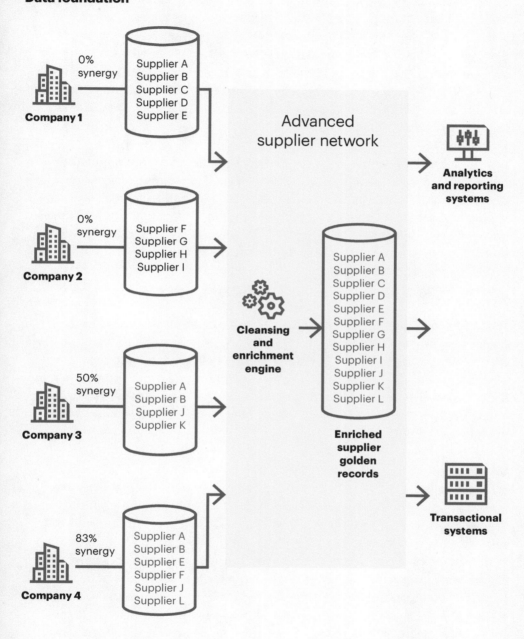

will consume all activity that a supplier engages in over the course of its life cycle. Thus, a proper data foundation will enrich every supplier record with risk, sustainability, and diversity measures so that it becomes easy to find new suppliers, new diverse suppliers, or report on spend by any of these dimensions. In short, data foundation provides a single source of truth for supplier data and in the process makes it easy to find diverse suppliers through "the network effect." The network effect pools assets across companies (in this case data) and creates synergies that benefit all participants that make use of the network.

Any company that buys access to a networked data foundation gets the benefit of all the other suppliers in the network. For example, if Pharma Company One signs up, the first thing it does is upload a file of all its suppliers. That list of suppliers goes through the cleansing and enriching process described above. Then Pharma Company Two signs up; it too will upload its supplier data. However, at this point there's probably a 70 percent overlap in the supplier lists, so the network only has to onboard 30 percent new suppliers.

When Pharma Company Three signs up, its supplier list will be 90 percent covered and by the time Pharma Company Four signs up there should be 99 percent coverage. This vastly simplifies the management and quality of supplier records. These records carry very granular levels of attribution that allow for precise filters and searching by various classifications, especially in diversity (for example, Black owned, women owned, LGBTQ owned, veteran owned, and so on).

Intelligence

When properly executed, the hub will give you the power to gain insights across all your procurement apps (connected by your data foundation). Imagine an Alexa or Siri interface that cuts across all apps and pulls the relevant data and analytics to make recommendations, take autonomous action, or simply do the bidding of the requestor. A good intelligence engine will be continuously learning from all the inputs, whichever app(s) they come from. For example, if an end user is looking at risk, they should be able to see the risk they're asking for, but also they should see relevant related risk they may not be aware of. This is equivalent to the Amazon recommended buying intelligence in which I search for a new iPad and it recommends accessories that other buyers like me have bought. The intelligence layer should track, recommend, predict, and execute across the entirety of the procurement value chain (see sidebar: The reach of the hub).

2.4.3 A new evaluation framework

The big question is: who provides this hub? This is the greatest gap right now. There are multiple ways to solve the hub problem. I have a number of clients whose IT groups have successfully built a bespoke hub and who are extremely happy with it. This approach has given them the power to add or subtract any procurement solution on their terms. Almost unbelievably one client I worked with can replace their procure-to-pay (P2P) system at will. This is a staggeringly impressive achievement and one I wouldn't have believed had I not seen it. Undoubtedly, some of the major S2P platforms will transform their offerings to hub systems (some are almost there). I also predict there will be new entrants into this space.

The reach of the hub

The spider chart should be the single biggest takeaway from this book. It represents the most fundamental shift in both how we think about digital procurement and, more importantly, how we structure our operating models. As noted throughout this text, the takeaway here is that if we are going to make procurement a truly digitally enabled function we need to better harness the power of technology and analytics. This means procurement practitioners have to embrace this, analysts have to change their evaluation models, systems integrators need to sell different types of projects, and strategists have to create new strategies and ways of operating.

Unless one is wedded to the failed state of the status quo it's safe to say most people see this as the path forward. However, the questions that remain are who will be the Salesforce of procurement and when will this become a reality? The answers to both are simply guesses at this point. But the spider chart, and the text in this book, are procurement's digital North Star.

Given the nuance and flexibility required in this new procurement value chain, you will have to change the way you evaluate procurement platforms and solutions. Six major criteria with corresponding sub-criteria form the basis of how these providers need to be evaluated:

1 **User experience.** Do procurement services go to where the user is? The provider must move beyond portals and catalogs. If we're not delighting the user, we're not doing it properly. If we have to do significant training sessions as part of the rollout, we're not doing it properly.

2 **Quality data.** Is supplier data fully harmonized and enriched? As Section 2.6.2 will explain in greater detail, data functions should also include cleansed transactional data, upstream/downstream data integration, and external inputs (signals, benchmarks, pricing, should-cost, and so on). We measure this success by the fact that we can publish a confidence score, give full transparency to the underlying data and rules, and create evidence that the data represents the single source of truth.

3 **Analytics.** Are analytics functions meaningful? Analytics is not dashboards or useless visualizations. As Section 2.6.2 will explain, true analytics tells us what we could be doing or what we should do. It gives us the optimal outcome. Useful analytics are prescriptive. So the generated insights need to feed and inform strategy.

4 **Automation.** Is there full automation of P2P, sourcing, and contracting? We measure this success by the ability to remove procurement people from the individual transaction level, the sophistication and speed at which we can support the business, and the value we can enable—and are we giving the user the best possible experience? Specifically, can we eliminate the buying desk, can we automate sourcing activities, or can we remove people from the reconciliation process?

5 **Ecosystem.** Can we build and sustain an ecosystem of third parties? We measure this success by the ease of use in employing best-of-breed technologies while ensuring data quality, security, and other business constraints are accounted for.

6 **Enablement of value creation.** If we achieve cost savings, can we trace it to EBITDA? If not, it's nothing more than monkey math. Can we generate value beyond cost savings? Are we contributing directly to the P&L? Are we driving ESG goals? Did we enable innovation?

Using these criteria, only two of the Big Six providers currently make the cut: Coupa and SAP Procurement. The others have a strategic challenge in front of them and, if unsuccessful, will start to slip down into serving mid-tier-sized companies that can effectively employ more discrete platforms, get acquired, or simply fade away. Undoubtedly there will be further market consolidation.

It's important to note that although the spider chart plots solutions to solve today's problems, the power of the ecosystem's central hub is that it will enable the development of tomorrow's solutions that haven't been built or even imagined.

2.4.4 A duopoly emerges?

Implicitly and seemingly, this means a duopoly with Coupa and SAP Procurement emerges. But more questions remain. Can Coupa and SAP Procurement effectively develop strategies and business models that will allow them to continue as a hub/platform provider? It's not a zero-sum game and the field is wide open. The biggest question is not if a third party will make a run at the prize, but who? Certainly, Workday has the potential given how it is building out its S2P ecosystem. Salesforce could view this as a viable endeavor—it's certainly well positioned having solved the commercial side of the business so why not the operations side? It has a track record of pursuing SRM-related activities, so why not go for a bigger piece of the pie? Why not buy one of the Big Six and really accelerate the effort? Or perhaps it's going to be one of the start-ups that decides it wants to make a big play.

2.4.5 New licensing models

The era of the $10 million, $20 million, or $30 million S2P projects is over. Not only did the big-bang approach fail to deliver, it's not relevant to how procurement operates. We have never been able to reconcile the legacy user-based model with the archetypes of business user, procurement user, supplier, executive, and ancillary function (legal, finance, and so on).

This is a good news/bad news situation. The good news is that with all the technological innovation, there is a whole host of new (or new versions of old) pricing models. This means that there is more flexibility in paying for these technologies. For example, a supplier-funded model means that cost is not an impediment to adopting a new technology. The bad news is that there is very little uniformity and potential conflict of interest in the licensing models. How do we charge a supplier for winning a sourcing event, but not charge them to be part of a supplier network that we use?

To sort through this complexity, we can look at what has worked in other domains. The Amazon Web Services (AWS) model, where we pay by consumption, is very successful. In the procurement world, this could be volume of spend, yield, percentage of savings—just to name a few. The supplier-funded model, where they pay if they're awarded business, may also work, although this approach is not applicable to all categories. Furthermore, it's marred by a long history of failed attempts, most notably the Ariba Supplier Network, where suppliers actively avoided participating in the network because the user interface was so bad and the returns elusive.

In the B2C market, the consumerization of enterprise software has arrived. Many of the greatest technological innovations originate from the consumer market. Apple's iOS (iPhone/iPad), Amazon (e-commerce), Netflix and YouTube (content generation and consumption), Wikipedia (knowledge capture), and Google (search) are just a few examples of breakthrough innovations in the consumer space. These solutions, and many like them, employ certain traits that allow them to become wildly popular with enormous user bases. These key traits of consumerized software are:

— Try before you buy

— Great UX

— Easy to use (no training required)

— Lightweight (no IT required)

— Intelligent (guide me to the right outcome)

Fair or not, business users view corporate technology solutions through the consumer lens. Most users can't understand how Twitter can provide real-time information exchange, but its financial reports or corporate purchasing tool take minutes to load, are painful to navigate, and fail to provide timely information. Companies often ask if users like a particular UX, but the proof is really in how much they use the tool and the ROI it generates. Additionally, we must remember that data is everything. All tech companies succeed by their ability to use and harness data across companies. It's data at scale that makes all the machine learning models work. And while some of that data comes back in aggregated format such as benchmarks, there are questions emerging in the consumer world surrounding the value of user-generated data that have implications for the corporate world. For example, if Facebook is making money from my interactions on the system by selling my data, should I receive monetary compensation? The same argument will eventually apply to enterprise software providers. In procurement, if I use a sourcing tool does that vendor have the right to use our company's data to improve its product, to make recommendations to other customers, or even extract the methodology and offer it to other clients? In other words, is a company's data more valuable than it's being given credit for? Could a particularly big enterprise trade its data for software licenses?

2.4.6 Why the central hub is powerful

We've been talking about the hub as both a software framework and a new way to conceptualize procurement. A fully developed hub will centralize data, create intelligence across all applications, offer seamless integration to the latest and greatest solutions, and provide a coherent, if not pleasurable, user experience. This will allow for precision in response to new business objectives with a primary focus on rapid time to value. This is important for a couple of reasons. First, you need to understand the concept before you run out and buy some software. If you don't have a deep understanding of what you want the software to do, you'll cede control to the vendors. The result will benefit them and not you. Second, this notion of reconceptualizing procurement operations has implications beyond the hub, throughout your entire operating model. The next few sections will illustrate how you apply this philosophy to your supplier ecosystem and your analytics capabilities.

By the way, I've been speaking primarily about large, private corporations. Scaled down, these lessons can apply to companies of any size. But if you're a nonprofit, or if you're in private equity, you may face special situations (see sidebars: Digital procurement for nonprofits; Digital procurement for private equity).

2.4.7 Rigid standardization versus personalization

To borrow a term from the consumerized world of technology, *personalization* is the concept that any technology I use needs to be customized to me. I want it to learn who I am, how I think, how I act. This is a sharp departure from the past whereby the way we used computers was strictly and rigidly controlled by Microsoft, IBM, Dell, and other computer providers. A Steve Jobs-led Apple brought color into the computing world, literally (and not for the first time) in 1999 when it rolled out five different colored iMacs. The blueberry, strawberry, lime, tangerine, and grape iMacs revolutionized the PC market with its histori-cally all-beige boxes known as PCs. These iMacs revealed consumers' latent desire for personalized technology.[2] This trend has accelerated over the past two decades and increasingly in recent years as machine learning has brought greater levels of personalization to users. Can you imagine an iPhone where you can only have the 12 apps that Apple wants you to have? And yet that is historically what S2P providers have given the procurement community.

When we think about procurement technology for the enterprise, we need to employ the same *personalization* concept. In this case, *personalization* represents the vast level of configuration required for each enterprise. Technology needs to be able to flexibly and seamlessly accommodate the nuance of every enterprise without costing tens of millions or taking an army of systems integrators. No two enterprises are the same, not even in the same industry, and most enterprises are in a continual state of evolution. This means there are few processes and technical requirements common across companies. So using a rigid set of tools is not successful, as we have learned. The *personalization* theme should cascade to the individual user. If I work in a manufacturing plant in Switzerland the system should know what I most commonly buy and from whom every time I log in to the system. It should

---

[2] Benj Edwards, "10 Years of Cuddly, Friendly iMacs," *Wired*, August 15, 2008, https://www.wired.com/2008/09/gallery-imac-anniversary/

Digital procurement for nonprofits

After one of my presentations I received a message from someone who asked me if all this fancy technology could be used for nonprofits. Simply, the answer is yes. Every procurement function needs the following foundational capabilities:

— Spend visibility

— P2P

— E-sourcing

— Contract repository

If you don't have these, the new innovative companies can help you get the capabilities enacted quickly and cheaply.

What comes next is where for-profit and nonprofits diverge a bit. For-profits need to look at an expansive array of sourcing, risk, SRM, and compliance/governance capabilities. This is because the scale of goods/services purchased creates the opportunity and need for management.

By contrast, most nonprofits don't have this scale especially considering that a lot of goods/services are in-kind donations (at least this was my experience). So all these fancy procurement tools have a different applicability. Can we use these tools to help us tap into new supply bases, improve sourcing capability, and drive spend through catalogs/group buying that gives you the benefit of volume discounts? Some specific examples:

— **Complex sourcing.** Using a sourcing tool to procure services. Cost savings generated through sourcing have a direct impact on a nonprofit's ability to deliver its core mission.

— **Contract analytics.** Preventing wasted money due to poorly worded or managed contracts is an absolute must. Also, this will help eliminate contract risk, which nonprofits can ill afford.

(continued on next page)

Digital procurement for nonprofits (continued)

— **Group purchasing.** Participating in group buying events. This concept hasn't taken off at the for-profit level for a variety of reasons. This is a huge benefit for nonprofits. I expect we'll see much more of these offerings in the years to come.

— **On-demand marketplaces.** Tools providing easy access and good pricing on a wide variety of goods and services. A quick way to manage cost and transparency.

— **Tail of tail.** Offloading the management and payment of low-value suppliers is a huge efficiency gain. This helps to avoid costly and lengthy onboarding/management.

— **Tail spend.** Nonprofits have a larger portion of tail spend than commercial companies so the ability to auto-source this spend at scale is a huge benefit.

— **Category solutions.** These solutions (for example, legal, marketing, print, facilities management, and so on) give immediate benefits that layer nicely on top of nonprofit operations.

know what my alternative suppliers are in the region and automatically calculate shipping, timing, tax, and inventory of whatever I need in advance of me asking for it. Amazon does this for consumers through a combination of intelligence, tracking, and *personalization*. It's time that procurement technology providers delivered this.

2.5 What comes next will truly transform procurement

Let's assume that the ecosystem comes to pass as defined above. What happens next? This is where a whole new procurement way of operating comes to pass.

Digital procurement for private equity

Broadly speaking, private equity (PE) firms buy distressed companies, infuse them with money, turn around the business operations, cut costs, and return the company to profitability as quickly as possible. As such, procurement has a prime role in delivering cost savings and operational efficiencies. In some cases, a portfolio company has no procurement capabilities, so everything is net new. In other cases, where procurement exists, companies are in their second or third generation of management where foundational procurement is in place but there's significant room for improvement. Regardless, the objective is the same: maximize cost savings now and make meaningful operational improvements. To that end, there are several key digital capabilities that need to be used.

In today's world, PE firms engage their portfolio companies with a range of procurement support. On the lighter side, they directly negotiate discounts with standard categories such as travel or perhaps office supplies. There are a few that team with group purchasing organizations (GPOs) to secure preferred pricing on a greater number of categories. On the heavier engaged side, PE firms have highly centralized and sophisticated procurement programs that require all portfolio companies to participate. Regardless of the degree of support that PE firms currently provide, with the evolution of digital procurement offerings there are even more opportunities to offer portfolio companies.

What is different for PE companies is that they can make enterprise investments that can then be leveraged (and charged back) across the portfolio companies. A meta spend cube—spend reporting across all the portfolio companies—is the most important asset a PE company can make. A central spend cube that holds the supplier's golden records and classification schemas ensures that reporting is consistent across the portfolio. Most meta spend cube providers offer the appropriate security and permissions to ensure that portfolio company spend data is viewed only by either the PE firm or portfolio company's senior leadership. For PE firms that have robust, centralized procurement programs, a meta spend cube is a necessary investment. When a new acquisition is made, its spend can be rapidly integrated into the central meta cube. PE firms

(continued on next page)

Digital procurement for private equity (continued)

benefit, especially during due diligence activity, from a rapid and clear insight into potential profitability and production of an opportunity assessment. Next up will be a P2P system to provide a logical way to manage spend. Again, a centralized approach to this will keep investment costs low and benefits high. This implementation should include setting up the various buying channels or a digital buy-desk. Streamlining this set of capabilities allows governance and control over how external expenditures are conducted.

Through the use of digitally enabled tools, PE firms and their portfolio company management teams can quickly track and manage spend. Highly commoditized categories such as general maintenance, repair, and operations (MRO), mobile telecom, office supplies, waste, and recycling make for great initial opportunities. For the advanced firm—including janitorial, utilities, temporary labor, and pack and ship—IT and hardware present big opportunities. Additionally, tail spend management solutions will enable scalable savings from auto-sourcing most spend.

From there simple and advanced sourcing (expressive bidding) capabilities will unlock a robust set of savings, depending on the types of categories and the spend volume. Finally, some basic level of contract analytics will be required. Some of this will be done through the acquisition phase. But one of the first steps should be to interrogate all the contracts for pricing and risk. These insights should feed the opportunity pipeline. A well-curated set of advanced digital sourcing tools will not only optimize market insights and data but also act as an enabler for portfolio company procurement professionals to shift the focus to more strategic human activity.

For many portfolio companies, priorities may not be in place to invest in procurement and analytic capabilities. There's a growing trend for PE firms to make additional investments to create a center of excellence and provide procurement as a service (PaaS). A PaaS offering is an on-demand procurement capability to provide procurement data analytics, execute optimization modelling, and conduct product tear-downs. This can be a crucial value driver to any firm especially for their small to medium-sized portfolio companies. Cost for PaaS services is reallocated by percent of benefit direct to the portfolio company or billed through annual subscription fees.

2.5.1 Next-generation sourcing: demand/supply matching

Demand/supply matching is the reincarnation of sourcing into a *market exchange* where supply and demand continuously meet and form prices. The market exchange will be 24/7, a continuous engine that will facilitate sourcing every single requisition because technology now makes this possible. This platform shows in real time the prices at which people are willing to buy or sell specific goods and services. In short, the Uberification of sourcing to match supply and demand in real time.

The exchange is an inevitable development given that transaction costs have been slashed, transparency can easily be created, and goods and services can be rapidly entered into the exchange. This means each individual company can choose to buy at the lowest price at any given moment, if they want to lock in specific price/quantity levels (for a fee, of course), or bespoke contracts and pricing for niche goods/services.

To expand market exchanges, and realize their benefits across the enterprise, procurement groups will need to take a greater role in specification management and demand forecasting, which is of course highly dependent on having good golden records. In fact, the key to participating, never mind successfully transacting, in the marketplace is the ability to have clear details on the particular buys. Consequently, the market exchange will force category/ commodity management to be exponentially more efficient and accurate.

Imagining the future sourcing marketing exchange isn't terribly hard as we just witnessed it come to life at the outset of COVID. As has been reported on extensively, early on in the pandemic the dearth of PPE became a crisis. A crisis that saw some companies with a glut of unused PPE collecting dust because their operations were shut down. Meanwhile, front-line operations in healthcare and first responders struggled to have adequate PPE. In response, new temporary solutions popped up that matched excess supply with critical demand. UPS partnered with supply chain solution provider Resilinc, Vecna Robotics, the federal government, and others to build one such exchange.[3]

---

[3] DC Velocity Staff, "UPS and Resilinc create hospital-to-hospital exchange for PPE—Covid-19 roundup for April 14," *DC Velocity*, April 14, 2020, https://www.dcvelocity.com/articles/45723-ups-and-resilinc-create-hospital-to-hospital-exchange-for-ppecovid-19-roundup-for-april-14

Kearney partnered with American Hospital Association, Kaiser Permanente, Merit Solutions, Microsoft, and UPS to build another such exchange.[4] The hallmark of this exchange was a dynamic supply and demand-matching algorithm. The algorithm identified where there was supply and matched it to the demand using modeling constraints (for example, location, criticality of need, severity of outbreak) to ensure equitable distribution. This proved that if there is sufficient need and desire, we can build new ways of technology-driven processes.

2.5.2 Next-generation requisitioning: rise of the productivity bot

Perhaps the most fundamental procurement service is to provide a clear, logical, and easy way for users to procure what they need. At least, that's the theory. Of course, most users don't experience it this way.

Yes, catalog management is difficult, but that's not an excuse for mediocre systems. These buying portals are based on procurement's ability to "manage" or at least give the perception of managing. What procurement is really trying to do is control the spend. But procurement is rarely successful in managing or controlling because the foundational design of these systems is based on the premise that user behavior can be distilled down, codified, and then built. Unfortunately, this doesn't work; user behavior cannot be predicted or codified, much less controlled. Therefore, procurement systems need to reverse the paradigm and give users flexibility and trust them to do the right thing. Thus, we enter the trust-but-verify paradigm.

Fundamentally, we need to design systems to bring procurement services to where the user is. Instead of users writing their brief or business case in Word and then having to cut and paste that into the requisition system, why don't we connect Word directly to the requisition system so that the requisition is automatically generated? We should be able to call up the Slackbot (or Teams equivalent) and ask it to requisition whatever it is that we need. The Slackbot should be able to handle everything end-to-end about each individual requisition.

---

[4] "Launching 'Protecting People Everywhere' to source PPE," Kaiser Permanente press release, April 14, 2020, https://about.kaiserpermanente.org/community-health/news/launching-protecting-people-everywhere-to-source-ppe

An articulation of this is illustrated in figure 10 on page 68. There are several key points to illuminate here. First, the SourceBot knows who the requisitioner is and what level of the organization they sit in, which confers the spending threshold. The SourceBot has knowledge of the category and subcategory in question (for example, print → 3D printing) and who the pre-qualified suppliers are. The SourceBot allows the user to easily suggest a supplier that is not in the system, correctly identifies the supplier contact information, and kicks off a background process to onboard them. Finally, once the purchase amount is stated the SourceBot knows that the amount is over the threshold, so it kicks off an approval workflow and tendering event once the supplier onboarding is complete. This example is taking the burden off the requisitioner as Tom simply has to make the initial ask and answer a few questions. The heavy burden of supplier identification, onboarding, approval, tendering, and award are done by the SourceBot—all activities that have historically been done by human procurement resources. This is exactly how we will eliminate the low-value transactional and operational procurement work. Moreover, it is important to note that there could be five to 10 solutions supporting this exchange alone, but the requisitioner never sees that. In fact, procurement wouldn't see that either as the entire requisition is handled by the SourceBot. This is why ecosystem complexity is not a long-term concern; no matter how many solutions/apps we employ they will largely sit in the background, accessed through smart interfaces.

2.5.3 Next-generation settlement/clearing: smart contracts

So far, we've looked at reimagining the sourcing and requisitioning processes and putting them into a new structure. But in both these cases we're elevating trends that have already been underway. But the extraordinary breakthrough will come when we can connect reimagined sourcing and requestioning processes and technologies to smart contracts.

For centuries, contracts have been paper documents that had ink-based signatures. As word processing came into existence, paper contracts evolved into digital documents. From there contract management systems were developed to offer features such as clause libraries, versioning, authoring, e-signature, and workflows, all of which extended the contract. However, despite all these features contract management in procurement has remained relatively immature and unadopted. According to the Global Contracting

Figure 10
Next Gen UX

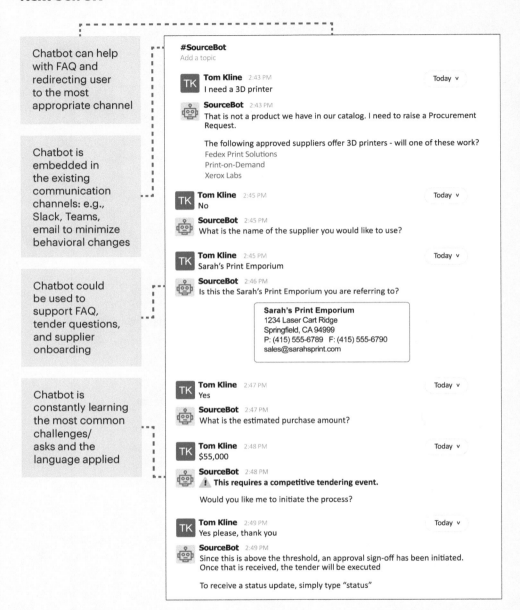

Chatbot can help with FAQ and redirecting user to the most appropriate channel

Chatbot is embedded in the existing communication channels: e.g., Slack, Teams, email to minimize behavioral changes

Chatbot could be used to support FAQ, tender questions, and supplier onboarding

Chatbot is constantly learning the most common challenges/ asks and the language applied

#SourceBot
Add a topic

Tom Kline 2:43 PM — Today ⌄
I need a 3D printer

SourceBot 2:43 PM
That is not a product we have in our catalog. I need to raise a Procurement Request.

The following approved suppliers offer 3D printers - will one of these work?
Fedex Print Solutions
Print-on-Demand
Xerox Labs

Tom Kline 2:45 PM — Today ⌄
No

SourceBot 2:45 PM
What is the name of the supplier you would like to use?

Tom Kline 2:45 PM — Today ⌄
Sarah's Print Emporium

SourceBot 2:46 PM
Is this the Sarah's Print Emporium you are referring to?

> **Sarah's Print Emporium**
> 1234 Laser Cart Ridge
> Springfield, CA 94999
> P: (415) 555-6789 F: (415) 555-6790
> sales@sarahsprint.com

Tom Kline 2:47 PM — Today ⌄
Yes

SourceBot 2:47 PM
What is the estimated purchase amount?

Tom Kline 2:48 PM — Today ⌄
$55,000

SourceBot 2:48 PM
⚠ **This requires a competitive tendering event.**

Would you like me to initiate the process?

Tom Kline 2:49 PM — Today ⌄
Yes please, thank you

SourceBot 2:49 PM
Since this is above the threshold, an approval sign-off has been initiated. Once that is received, the tender will be executed

To receive a status update, simply type "status"

Source: Kearney analysis

Management Association, most contracting features remain underutilized.[5] Regardless of these significant adoption gaps, there's a fundamental change that has occurred in contracting. We need to move from a paper document to a data construct. In other words, we need to stop managing contracts as documents and start managing them as data entities.

Once contracts become data objects, that opens up a whole world of possibilities. Historically, contracting in procurement has belonged to the *upstream* part of the procurement process, while payment was in the *downstream* part of the process—there was a logical and often technical separation between the two functions. And yet is it possible for them to be decoupled? The short answer is no. Why on earth would one want to negotiate a contract that wasn't directly connected to delivery and payment?

Enter the *smart contract*, which takes the relevant contract data and programmatically ties all the terms and conditions to consumption/delivery of the goods and services—when the conditions are met, the contract releases payment. In some cases, such as IT platforms or software as a service, the contract can be programmatically tied to the transactional system, which further streamlines payments and performance. For example, let's imagine we contract with a software provider that promises 99.999 percent uptime with a clause specifying that failure to achieve this triggers a 10 percent discount. In this case, somebody has to monitor the reports to see if the specified service is adhered to and if not begin a manual review process and notification back to the vendor. With a smart contract, that process looks totally different. The contract clause around performance can be programmed to monitor the SLA metrics (from the operational system) and when an outage drops to a level where the discount kicks in, the system can automatically apply the discount to the monthly charge, or if it's an annual charge a refund request can be automatically triggered. With smart contracts, we can also systematically execute discounts and penalties, either automatically or with human review. This systematizes and streamlines activities that are today either poorly managed or managed with great cost and effort. In other words, the smart contract is not just a technological toy. It requires us to change the organizational construct of how we contract and pay.

[5] According to the International Association for Contract & Commercial Management Benchmark Report 2019, p. 27

Smart contracts have the advantage of being flexible. This means that in the midst of a crisis, they can be reprogrammed to adjust payment terms, moving them forward or pushing them out or paying a premium. Because the contract and payment functions are tied together, you and your business gain the ability to adjust on the fly. This of course makes compliance real-time and fully auditable. That alone is a huge win. Moreover, performance tracked through a smart contract can be used upstream in supply/demand matching. Performance can be used to influence awarding of business.

Of course, today you can use contract analytics to streamline the complexity and proliferation of contracts. If we have 1,000 contracts, we can use analytics to easily see the variance between clauses. We gain two benefits:

— We can quickly see where we might have mismatched payment terms or unaccounted-for risk.

— When we identify needless complexity, we can use intelligence to build new contracts, which can automatically be validated against our preferred terms. This means we have fewer touch points with legal, so we can improve our SLAs.

These activities go away automatically with a smart contract because they become embedded in the programmatic logic.

Over the past few years, a three-way match process has emerged. It matches invoices to the PO and the goods received. (Sometimes it's a four-way match, including quality information.) This is fine for goods, but what happens when we're buying more complex goods, such as those that are services-based? In these cases, we have complex SLAs specified in the contract. They require compliance checkoffs, performance, discounting thresholds, payment execution, and payment moderation.

We need more sophisticated contract management systems that incorporate this three-way match process, tying together the contract, the performance, and the payment. This need will only increase, because estimates place the balance of a company's spend on services at over 50 percent.[6] This is the value of the smart contract: by tying everything together, it streamlines these activities, and in the process it changes the construct of the entire S2P process.

Arguably, we need to deconstruct P2P systems and use smart contracts as the organizing construct. In other words, we use the contract to automatically manage the order–receive–reconcile–pay process. Then we use sophisticated new technologies to vastly improve the requisitioning process, including both directs that come from ERP systems and indirects that come from requests in myriad channels (see figure 11 on page 72).

The figure shows a high level of how this smart contracting construct works. The center of the image highlights the core functions to manage the entire contract life cycle as data (not a document). Again, because it's data driven it's straightforward to accept data from sourcing, quality, and other functional systems that either inform the contract creation or make use of the contracted terms (for example, pushing price information into the ERP system). Further, the contract terms can be tied into the P2P to manage performance and payment (as described above).

2.6 Procurement analytics

Ask consultants or technology vendors to define *procurement analytics*, and you might be both shocked and disappointed with the answers. Many begin with a nod to artificial intelligence (AI), machine learning, and big data. Then they throw in a combination of spend visibility, data rationalization, bid optimization, savings tracking, and benchmarking. You might also receive the oblique response that analytics enables a category strategy. Although all these are good activities, they don't provide an adequate definition.

---

[6] An amalgamated number from: Gartner, Everest, TPI, Evalueserve, Research and Markets, Zinnov, Global Industry Analysts Inc., and Transport Intelligence as compiled by SirionLabs

Figure 11
Smart contract construct

Enterprise systems   Business requirements

Sourcing systems	**ERP systems**	**Quality systems**	**Quality requirements**	**EHS requirements**	**Legal requirements**
↑↓	↑↓	↑↓	↓	↓	↓

Smart contracts

Identification	**Authoring**	**Iteration**	**Execution**	**Records management**	**Ongoing management**	**Reporting/ analytics**

↑↓	↑↓	↑↓	↑↓

Obligation/goods management	**Invoicing/PO**	**Payment**	**Relationship management**
— SLAs	— Consumption	— Requisition to pay	— Issues
— Rate cards	— Claims	— Disputes	— Risks
— Price adjustment	— Credits/ earn-backs	— Payment	— Compliance/ audits

Source: Kearney analysis

Simply put, procurement analytics is the ability to provide a single source of truth for all supplier and commodity data and turn that data into automated, proactive, applied intelligence. Good procurement analytics enables three business objectives:

1 Analytics improves supplier engagement by providing insights to move from one-off price haggling to collaborating for improvements and new opportunities.

2 Analytics increases transparency into supplier performance management. Suppliers almost always know more about you than you know about them, and negative information asymmetry puts you at a disadvantage.

3 Analytics is the foundation for a robust risk management program that not only identifies risk, but also recommends ways to mitigate that risk. This involves going beyond individual supplier health to consider the broader supply market, alternative suppliers, and what-if scenario planning.

2.6.1 Spend cubes are an intellectual trap

As you probably know, when you construct a spend cube, you take every transaction in which your company spends money (invoices, credit cards, and so on) and put them into a format that shows how much you're spending, where, and with whom (including with companies that are owned by bigger companies). The spend cube will show you how much you spend with your management consultancy company or your top 10 suppliers in China.

Many companies struggle to get to this level of reporting. So they undertake subpar initiatives to build spend cubes—sometimes in-house, sometimes with consultants, and sometimes with traditional S2P vendors (this was one of the S2P vendor value propositions that failed spectacularly).

Spend cube initiatives are not opportunities; they're a plea for help. Although knowing where money has been spent is mildly useful as a starting point for sourcing and taking corrective action, it's a backward-looking perspective that's rarely integrated with financial reports and a general ledger that tracks corporate performance. For indirect spending, the problem is even more difficult, as many transactions lack the requisite line-item details in a format that makes sense. More importantly, spend cubes identify only where the money was spent. Once the money is spent, it's non-recoverable. Often, that money has gone to unsanctioned suppliers, off-contract, or where the supplier didn't meet the negotiated terms.

Spend cubes are part of "smash-and-grab" procurement. Well-intentioned people (both internal and external) or technology companies swoop in and analyze spend data. They find easy opportunities to negotiate savings. Then they plant the flag of success, noting the "millions of dollars of savings." The problem is that all these so-called savings are theoretical: they may happen, but they may not, due to a variety of unforeseen issues. Moreover, smash-and-grab procurement has become the de facto standard for procurement initiatives. This is why it's so important to get back to the fundamentals of procurement.

If you can't solve spend visibility in three weeks, you're doing it wrong. But the answer isn't to demand that new spend cube initiatives have three-week horizons. The answer is to reset your approach to procurement analytics.

2.6.2 Start with the foundation

Good procurement analytics requires a clean, accessible single source of truth for all supplier information—the data foundation. However, to truly do procurement analytics we must build a centralized procurement data lake (PDL). Regardless of the underlying technology, a PDL provides a straightforward, logical place to store all supplier, transaction, and commodity information. This information then drives proactive insight generation and automation especially in the context of broader supply chain analytics (see sidebar: Building an effective data lake).

Leading companies are well down the road in their PDL progress. For those that are just starting or are experiencing problems, the good news is that building and maintaining a PDL is most often done in partnership with IT once the core requirements are defined. Procurement need not carry the operational burden. Companies that don't have PDL capabilities can partner with start-ups that can create one as well as existing technology companies that can streamline data curation.

Building an effective data lake

A data lake is a storehouse for raw data. Think of it as a large pool that can be filled with all types of data, regardless of format (see figure 12 on page 76). As the figure shows, this is where all procurement data is (ERP, P2P, and so on). Sitting above the data is a series of data governance and management capabilities. Finally, there are different user personas that have different data access requirements that need to be accommodated.

However, the existence of a data lake doesn't mean that you should pour all your data into it. Building an effective data lake takes careful planning to ensure the following capabilities:

— Accommodate structured and unstructured data.

— Enable real-time and near-real-time data updating and access.

— Handle the expanding requirements for data complexity, speed, and size.

— Automate extract, transform, and load processes.

— Allow for external data integrations.

— Use microservices for point-to-point integration.

— Be capable of dynamically adding data sources.

— Be able to retrieve and manipulate data without technical details or knowing where the data is located.

— Have federated data with minimized replication.

— Establish a golden record and segmentation of data.

— Create one standard enrichment process to identify the most effective use of resources (cleansing and harmonization) and external feeds.

Figure 12
Building an effective data lake

User groups

| **Business user** (upstream/ downstream) | **Procurement** | **Bot** | **Supplier** | **Leadership** (procurement, business, cross function) |

Procurement data lake

Structured   **Unstructured**

Security and access control

Modeling and visualization

API services

Key harmonization

Other services

Data management	**ERP systems**	**P2P systems**	**Spend**	**SRM**	**External feeds**
— Supplier golden records	— Direct supply chain	— Payment	— Data feed 1	— SRM tool 1	— Financial risk
	— Indirect supply chain	— Requisition	— Data feed 2	— SRM tool 2	— News
	— Other systems	— Contract-ing	— Data feed 3	— SRM tool 3	— Social media
		— ...			— Regulatory
					— Market indices

Source: Kearney analysis

Data curation is a core component of a PDL. Procurement needs to be able to clearly identify for IT (or another responsible party) the important and relevant data, how it should be transformed, and the necessary SLAs for updating and accuracy. Specifically, how should suppliers be categorized, can suppliers be in multiple categories, how will parenting issues be resolved, and how should suppliers that are also competitors or consumers be flagged? These are just a sampling of the types of requirements that procurement must not only specify, but also own and maintain. Thus, procurement must have a strong, active partnership with IT along with dedicated resources to be equal partners in the building and ongoing maintenance and governance of the PDL.

2.6.3 Start using analytics to generate useful insights

With clean data and advanced analytics (such as data mining, predictive modeling, simulation, and optimization), procurement can generate meaningful insights and practical information that will tip the supply and demand power into the hands of the buyer. Specifically, the generated insights should feed directly to category managers and into the downstream sourcing and requisition systems.

Procurement analytics should reveal the answer to the following questions:

— Do I understand what I want to buy and in what quantity?

— How do I get the best deal for what I want to buy?

— What is the best deal?

— Am I choosing from and dealing with the right set of suppliers?

— Are my chosen suppliers delivering what I think I am buying?

— Am I getting what I contracted from my suppliers?

— Are my own internal stakeholder needs being met?

A category manager's job is to enable a business to turn supply market capabilities into value for end customers. To do this, they must build in the right sourcing and specification decisions at the point of purchase, combined with a closed-loop system to track supplier performance and improve decision-making. In practical terms, a category manager needs this in-depth data to assess what's happening in a particular supply market at any given time: changes in commodity prices, risk factors (such as *E. coli* outbreaks, tariffs, or other disruptions), supplier performance, new supplier identification, dynamic supplier segmentation, benchmarks, historical bids, and cost to serve. This information can be used to scenario-plan from a forward-looking point of view to identify all potential outcomes. For example, what are the strategy trade-offs between service level, cost, inventory, freight, and project cost?

The ability to see the available options then allows category managers to find the best outcome and decide whether to insource or outsource, automate, do a joint venture, or make other decisions that can affect EBITDA. For example, a forward-looking category manager can use advanced analytics to derive deep category insight that goes beyond solely spend analysis. This would enable two changes.

First, breaking down products into their individual components creates price transparency, allowing the buyer and supplier to use mutually agreed-upon cost formulas and eliminating the need for extensive negotiations. More importantly, this allows category managers to spend their time on value-added services such as risk mitigation and opportunities for growth and innovation. Similarly, category managers should build should-cost models that are based on supplier inputs such as manufacturing efficiencies, conversion time, labor rates, and raw material pricing. Because more external vendors are offering should-cost modeling services and benchmarks, outsourcing might be a cost-effective option depending on the category. In both examples, these analytic approaches free up category managers to do their job effectively.

Second, good procurement analytics can help predict spend by category. For instance, if an external workforce category manager wants to predict spend, he or she could combine a demand forecast with benchmarked wage rates versus commission rates and supplier performance. Armed with this information, the category manager can run a better sourcing event with specification and SLA optimization.

Analytics does not obviate the need for classic skills such as negotiations and the ability to determine a sourcing strategy based on supply and demand power. What it does do is complement those tools so they can be deployed more effectively. However, the cart should not come before the horse. Analytics should be based on the specifics of the category. For example, some organizations make cost models mandatory for all categories—regardless of the supply and demand drivers and the sourcing strategy. This is a classic case of analytics being used for its own sake. Cost models have a valuable role, but that role must be part of a category strategy, not an end in itself.

Beyond improving category strategies, the long-term opportunity is the ability to generate differentiated proactive and forward-looking insights that enable actions that do not need human intervention. Think automated bots that can operate autonomously in response to automatically generated analytic insights. For example, forward-looking risk management evaluates financial, security, location, raw material, corporate responsibility, regulatory, and operational risk (see figure 13). Inputs for each of these components can

Figure 13
Framework for active risk

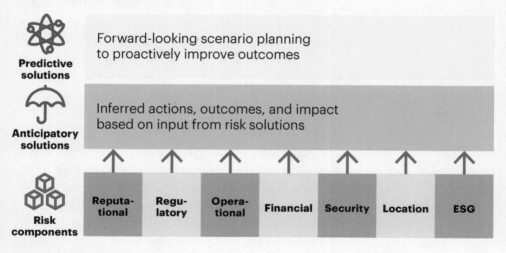

Source: Kearney analysis

come from many different external inputs—more than one person can efficiently process and act on. However, an automated bot can continually evaluate the risk profile across the entire value chain. If a particular risk threshold is identified, then an automated set of actions can be kicked off, including conducting a sourcing event to proactively change the supplier mix—all without direct human interaction.

Ultimately, strategic insights done well will enable category managers, who are located with the product lines, to walk into any product meeting and provide historical spend in that category, identify the contracted suppliers, show supplier bidding activity (including those that were not awarded business), alternative suppliers, external benchmarks, commodity pricing, risk profiles, corporate responsibility, trends in that particular category, and even should-cost models. All of this should be generated in a timely fashion and be available at a category manager's fingertips without having to rely on vast amounts of spreadsheets or an army of analysts. This is what an effective supplier and category 360-degree view will produce. In the process, it will open up a supply and demand advantage, optimize costs, and mitigate risk.

2.7 Digitally enabled environmental, social, and governance

COVID-19 hit the relatively unprepared business world like an unexpected volcano eruption and completely disrupted business operations. Unfortunately, other events over the course of 2020 also reshaped how companies think about environmental, social, and governance (ESG). Until 2020, ESG meant some tepid moves on sustainability, nominal nods to diversity, and the championing of causes such as Women's History Month, Black History Month, and Pride. Initiatives were chock-full of staged photo ops that looked good for the annual report but did little to ameliorate the problems facing the global citizenry.

One of the lasting legacies of 2020 will be how ESG jumped to the top of the corporate strategic objectives. The laissez-faire approach to ESG is no longer tenable amid massive social upheaval. As individual brands seek to sell to a more socially conscious demographic (Millennials and younger), companies must put greater effort into how they produce products, reduce their environmental impact, and create meaningful social change. In other words, to reach their targeted demographics, corporations must step in to fill a gap created as governments abdicate their social responsibility. However, this becomes a huge problem for procurement because many of our n-tier suppliers are located at or near sites of unstable political upheavals.

In an alarming number of cases, a national government is simply a failed state (such as, most recently, Myanmar). Nongovernmental organizations such as the United Nations, World Bank, and the World Health Organization are under severe political attack. In response, corporations are stepping in to fill the void. In fact, corporations have become so involved that there's now pushback from activists against corporations becoming too involved in social issues. For example, in advance of Pride each year there's usually a public questioning of whether Pride Month is selling out to corporations.[7] In 2018, *Vox* carried an article entitled "How LGBTQ Pride Month became a branded holiday," in which the author challenges whether corporate support of Pride is merely part of a branding campaign. The article notes that, for example, Adidas has a "Pride pack" of Pride merchandise readily available for sale. Simultaneously, Adidas was a major sponsor of the 2018 World Cup held in Russia, a country that is continually hostile and punishing to queer people. If money spent on Adidas merchandise ends up supporting the Russian government and its persecution of the queer community, then Adidas is not serving its queer customers well. Good ESG is complicated. This is part of a trend of "greenwashing," "rainbow washing," or "woke washing," whereby corporations purportedly make efforts in support of ESG but simultaneously make ethical trade-offs in pursuit of profit. Naturally, balancing these competing objectives is hard where weighing a passionate customer base against shareholders' interests leads to alienating one or both constituencies. Thus, any opportunity to advance ESG while maximizing profit—something procurement is well positioned to influence—will be warmly received.

As figure 14 on page 82 shows, procurement is in a good position to spearhead corporate ESG, because its work with external suppliers and entities sits at the intersection of an enterprise's environmental, social justice, consumer safety, human rights, and diversity, equity, and inclusion efforts (DE&I).

---

[7] *Vox's* "How LGBTQ Pride Month became a branded holiday," *Mashable's* "Dear Corporate America, leave our LGBTQ Pride celebrations alone," and *The Washington Post's* "Pride for sale," to name a few

Figure 14
The ESG Venn diagram

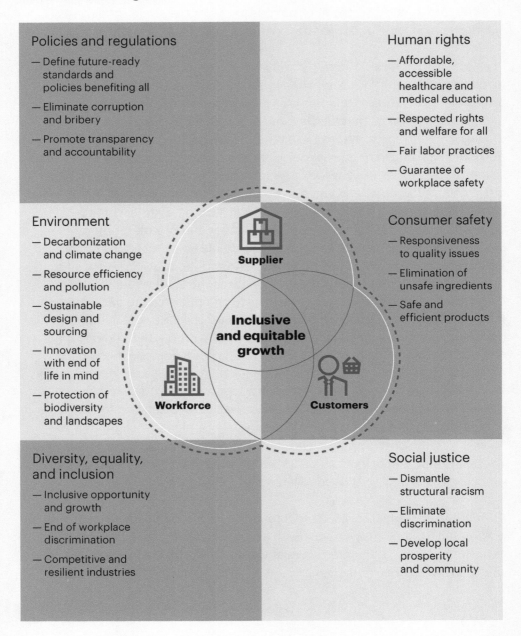

Policies and regulations
— Define future-ready standards and policies benefiting all
— Eliminate corruption and bribery
— Promote transparency and accountability

Human rights
— Affordable, accessible healthcare and medical education
— Respected rights and welfare for all
— Fair labor practices
— Guarantee of workplace safety

Environment
— Decarbonization and climate change
— Resource efficiency and pollution
— Sustainable design and sourcing
— Innovation with end of life in mind
— Protection of biodiversity and landscapes

Consumer safety
— Responsiveness to quality issues
— Elimination of unsafe ingredients
— Safe and efficient products

Supplier

Inclusive and equitable growth

Workforce

Customers

Diversity, equality, and inclusion
— Inclusive opportunity and growth
— End of workplace discrimination
— Competitive and resilient industries

Social justice
— Dismantle structural racism
— Eliminate discrimination
— Develop local prosperity and community

Source: Kearney analysis

Procurement can influence—and in some cases require—suppliers to use sustainable materials, employ fair labor practices, and be compliant with basic human rights. But procurement can extend further by looking at suppliers' workforce composition, diversity of ownership, or the ESG expectations to be met by their suppliers' suppliers. In other words, by employing ESG across the supply base it's possible to create an exponential gain of benefits.

2.7.1 Supplier diversity

For the better part of summer 2020, companies took seriously the long-standing issue of racial injustice and police brutality against the Black community in America and select other countries. These events further changed the political, social, and business landscape by serving notice that passivity was no longer an option. Diversity is not a choice.

We live in a "cancel culture," where complacent behavior can lead to an exodus of customers. Starbucks learned this lesson the hard way. On June 9, Starbucks issued a memorandum to its employees prohibiting Black Lives Matter (BLM) pins and T-shirts. The company was met with a vociferous backlash calling for boycotting of the global coffee chain. Three days later Starbucks relented and removed its exclusion of BLM clothing representations. Sadly, Starbucks is not new to controversy regarding the Black community. Two years ago in Philadelphia two Black men, Rashon Nelson and Donte Robinson, were denied access to the bathroom at a local Starbucks. The manager called 911 and had Nelson and Robinson arrested. This led to the company shutting every store for company-wide racial bias training.

Stories about cancel culture often quickly become political. People want to *judge* Starbucks as either an unfairly targeted victim or an evil expression of institutionalized racism. But that's not my point in telling this story. The point is that living in a world of cancel culture can be expensive. In that context, a company's supply base represents significant reputational risk that can feed into cancel culture dynamics. For example, if a tier 4 supplier engages in forced labor and gets caught, it's the brand itself that takes the reputational hit. This extends to supplier diversity as well. As supply chains become more transparent to consumers there's an expectation that a company's suppliers and its suppliers' suppliers have adequate diversity in their ownership, leadership, and workforces. Thus, any procurement organization needs to be hyper-focused on the diversity of its entire supply base because consumers and competitors are keeping score.

Regardless of your political feelings, cancel culture is likely not going away. In the era of hyper-transparency-based social media, cancel culture in reaction to social issues remains a great threat and lever for changing bad policies. Consumers want to know where brands stand on issues of diversity and social justice. Generations Y and Z rightly expect brands to be part of the solution. Consequently, every enterprise will need to develop its own strategy and response to the pressing issue of diversity. The power of procurement is that it often controls large portions of the external spend, which means it can employ tools and surface insights that will contribute to a company's diversity goals. In other words, when it comes to ESG, procurement can influence significant change by wielding its expertise and control.

In practical terms, moving the needle on supplier diversity starts at the top with the CEO and board making bold commitments. From there it is incumbent upon the procurement leadership to take responsibility for meaningful diverse supplier engagement. It is the vast array of digital tools that eliminate excuses for not using diverse suppliers. With this context, let's take a closer look at how procurement can move the needle on supplier diversity.

The data foundation in action
The most obvious opportunity for procurement to make a difference is implementing a focused effort to increase spend with diverse suppliers.

But the question remains: how to find diverse suppliers? The easiest answer is to employ a good data foundation (described in Section 2.4.2). This is where the power of the hub flexes its muscle. The data foundation contains cleansed and enriched data that allows procurement to easily identify diverse suppliers in day-to-day procurement operations. This eliminates the common excuse, "We don't know how to find diverse suppliers." Inviting diverse suppliers opens up both competition and the possibility of identifying new capabilities.

The power of using the data foundation is that the supplier records can then be syndicated to downstream systems such as sourcing and requisitioning. This is where procurement can really move the needle on bringing more spend to the table. Having access to a good supplier network allows for the identification and invitation of diverse suppliers to sourcing events. Then during the sourcing process diverse suppliers can be factored into different award scenarios so that a predefined portion of spend goes to diverse suppliers.

Further downstream in the requisitioning process, a good P2P system tied to the supplier network above will give requisitioners the option to effect a diverse choice when making a requisition. And when end users don't award to a diverse supplier or make a diverse choice, the opportunity cost is calculated and flagged for the diversity compliance officer. All these examples are the minimum actions a company could and should take.

But better processes are not enough. There is a massive requirement for more diverse suppliers in these networks. Good supplier networks should be measured against the number of diverse, quality suppliers they onboard and maintain. This need is ever more crucial where data emerging from the COVID crisis identifies that 41 percent of Black-owned businesses closed in April 2020 alone.[8] This is where organizations such as the National Minority Supplier Development Council and Women's Business Enterprise National Council will continue to play a vital role beyond certification. These organizations are involved directly in the community to identify and onboard diverse suppliers, cultivating a pipeline of new suppliers. The change here is that these organizations can leverage the power of the supplier networks to amplify their work. Further, companies can leverage supplier networks to make their spend reporting illuminate spend by diverse supplier. Specifically, by having enriched supplier records, once a company's spend data is added then an accurate and comprehensive reporting of diversity is available instantaneously. With this greater visibility, companies can work proactively, using the methods above, to adjust their spend as they go.

More advanced ways of moving the needle
Another example of work that matters is proactive supplier intervention. A procurement group that employs a good supplier performance system will be able to track and measure diverse supplier performance and proactively

---

[8] Aaron Ross Coleman, "Study: Covid-19 lockdowns hit black-owned small businesses the hardest," *Vox*, June 10, 2020, https://www.vox.com/2020/6/10/21286759/study-covid-19-lockdowns-black-owned-businesses-hardest-recession

(and even predictively) monitor performance to intercede if problems are detected to help avoid losing contracts.

The price for a supplier to onboard with most large enterprises is high. Not only is it costly but it also requires significant investment of time and is onerous to manage. Quixotically, these are the same enterprises that can truly effect the necessary changes by awarding contracts to the suppliers they burden with complex onboarding requirements. Thus, it's not hard to see how this becomes an impediment to engaging diverse suppliers (the same is true for start-ups as part of innovation initiatives): legal agreements that are denser and harder to read than *War and Peace*, security audit and compliance reviews that Google or Amazon probably could not pass (consisting of useless requirements that exist to ensure IT somehow remains relevant), jumping through extra hoops to be in preferred supplier programs, and generally signing away one's free will and participation in democracy. These require-ments, while perhaps well intentioned, have a chilling effect on onboarding diverse (and small) suppliers. They become self-defeating for corporations that want to engage more diverse suppliers but make it absurdly hard to do.

There are two opportunities to solve the seeming lack of diversity in supply bases. First, enterprises can work to build diverse supplier programs that streamline and standardize the rules of engagement for onboarding and engagement. Similarly, purveyors of data foundations could provide a similar service. They could have pre-accepted contract clauses, intelligent security checks, and pre-accepted or streamlined rules of engagement. On the buy side, the same technology that enables group buying functionality could be used here. If buyers can dynamically pool their resources to make purchases, why can suppliers not use the same concepts in a supplier network/P2P system; pool their resources to simplify onboarding. Finally, another opportunity to engage and retain diverse suppliers could be to offer early pay options, shorter payment terms, or supply chain financing with lower interest rates.

2.7.2 Sustainability

Fighting global warming and doing right by the world isn't new. It's not merely virtue signaling. And it's not some innovation created by the international elite at Davos. Automobile pioneer Henry Ford was an early and serious believer in "industrial conservation" or what's these days termed *sustainability*. Ford didn't like production waste. He invested a huge effort to increase efficiency and reusability within the factory. One example—which portended today's circular economies—was the creation of a "disassembly line" that took junked cars and recycled the materials to be used in new car production. Unfortunately, this effort proved to be too costly and was eventually abandoned. That's a trend all too common in today's supply chains, where what's good for the environment isn't always perceived as good for the near-term bottom line. But we can change that, especially within procurement, because money talks.

Sustainability has been a back-burner objective, background white noise, for far too long. Sustainability benefits historically haven't been immediately evident, often being seen as taking years to make meaningful change. But that is shifting. Consider that Company A may spend millions of dollars to haul and dump trash in a landfill each year. Each load of trash affects the community surrounding the landfill, contributing to poor quality of life, toxic materials leeching into the ground water, and increased localized greenhouse gas emissions. However, if we consider the true value, we might be throwing away perfectly good materials that can, with a little modification, act as an input to another production system and become a revenue source, a veritable trash-to-cash opportunity.

In the era of hyper-transparency, companies need to move beyond the traditional, tepid ESG mandate of "do no harm." Tomorrow's supply chains need to put environmental impact front and center. Consumers are increasingly demanding it and governments will eventually do so too. Most consumers can see that global climate change is real and it's having tangible impacts on their purchasing decisions. For example, Unilever reported that its sustainable brands grew 46 percent faster than traditional ones.[9] This trend points to the need for efficient manufacturing, packaging, and delivery. So supply chains need to be aware of these trends.

For example, consider a medical device provider that packages its products using sterilized plastic. Its consumers may demand more sustainable practices. Or certain shareholders may demand an improved sustainability score. Either

---

[9] "Unilever's Sustainable Living Plan continues to fuel growth," Unilever press release, October 5, 2018, https://www.unilever.com/news/press-releases/2018/unilevers-sustainable-living-plan-continues-to-fuel-growth.html

way, shifting that packaging to biodegradable plastic would be a big win. So the question is whether procurement can quickly and efficiently find a supplier that can deliver biodegradable plastic—and if not, then how does the company find a partner to collaborate to develop it? In either case, it's likely the incumbent supplier may not have a readily available solution so instead of purely focusing on the cost, the problem equation now gets focused on innovation. This is no longer simply a cost savings exercise— instead it's a true measure of procurement's ability to create value.

Companies that build physical products are faced with the fundamental question of whether to use raw materials extracted from the ground or figure out how to use recycled materials. This quickly becomes a trade-off in terms of cost, quality, and manufacturing process. But if we can tie that back to creating a more commercially viable product that consumers will pay a premium for, then the entire cost equation changes.

Globally, multiple CEOs are committing that their enterprises will go net zero by as soon as 2025; the question now becomes how to achieve these goals. As a savvy CPO, you might sense the opportunity (or seize the moment) and raise your hand to sign up to deliver 50 percent of that commitment. As the person who has influence over the company's entire external spend, you and your organization can influence significant results toward that goal. Not only that, but you have some big (if not obvious) levers to pull, that will drive benefits exponentially. These levers are requisitioning, sourcing, digitalization, and operations.

2.7.3 Forced labor and conflict minerals

Perhaps the greatest gap identified by COVID-19 was the lack of n-tier visibility in supply chains. This lack of visibility meant that companies struggled to map their risk effectively. When it comes to forced labor and conflict minerals the same issue applies. Do you know how your suppliers' suppliers are treating their suppliers? How are conditions at the farm level where cotton is grown? How are conditions in the mines where minerals are extracted?

Often, when it comes to supply chain risk management, the higher the risk the lower the visibility. Simply sending a survey to the tier 1/2/3 supplier is not good enough because what happens at the source is not visible to the upstream suppliers, much less the brand. When transparency evaporates, workers become vulnerable to abusive situations. The solution here is multifaceted. First, digital tools can certainly help with the scale and monitoring of these problems by doing extensive live scanning of news, government publications, NGOs, and social media. The ability to quickly and intelligently monitor and process potential risks (risk signaling) is a crucial, yet very basic, step in addressing this. To contextualize this, when talking about n-tier risk, digital solutions only solve a minimal part of problem. When we're talking about forced labor (FL) and conflict minerals (CM) in particular, these usually occur in regions where bribery is common and governments are lackadaisical at best in their enforcement of human rights. News and information emerging from these countries is opaque, often controlled and/or censored by the government itself, thus neutering the efficacy of digital tools. And sometimes governments float in and out of failed states, making accurate intelligence gathering and response planning a complete guessing game. So any good risk management capability that seeks to address FL and CM needs a comprehensive response that covers both digital tools to look at the macro picture and a boots-on-the-ground approach at the tail end of the supply chain.

Recently, Outland Denim, an international fashion brand, sought to do more to ensure that its suppliers complied with human rights standards by developing an even stronger social image. The brand partnered with PSG, a boots-on-the-ground intelligence solutions provider, to address the difficult challenges of supply chain traceability that numerous clothing companies across industries worldwide are facing. The pair developed a comprehensive communication strategy to solicit feedback from the most vulnerable worker tiers in the deepest level of their supply chain, which were the unregulated cotton farms. The strategy consisted of posters, newspaper postings, television, radio broadcasts, and use of social media. This on-the-ground system allowed the farm workers to quickly communicate concerns or instances of exploitation directly to PSG as an intermediary so it could investigate conditions on the ground and then raise remediation opportunities to the supplier and upstream in the supply chain all the way back to the brand itself. Examples of worker complaints included lack of clean water, wage disputes, access to personal protective equipment, and living conditions. Another advantage of the boots-on-the-ground approach was that information sourced from workers outside of the workplace, rather than through a supplier feedback or grievance mechanism, had a higher level of integrity and proved to be highly actionable.[10]

It is important to note that the network effect can work here as well. Not every enterprise has to put boots on the ground, something that could unintentionally backfire; instead this can be done through consortiums by commodity and geography. Most digital devices use as core raw materials a fair amount of cassiterite (for tin), wolframite (for tungsten), coltan (for tantalum), and gold ore. These minerals are mostly mined from the Democratic Republic of Congo (DRC). Since achieving independence from Belgium in 1960, the DRC has experienced a series of politically destabilizing events, wars, and coups. There is a long history of human rights violations associated with the DRC. But the DRC is rich in the minerals that power the digital era. As one might expect, tech companies are heavily invested in tracking and preventing these human rights violations. However, as an example, if you are a medical device or automotive manufacturer, chances are that you're using a significant number of electronic components and you may not have the visibility into these aspects. This is where tying into consortiums by commodity or region can have an exponential impact; you get the benefits by working with those that have a vested interest. For instance, companies in the high-tech space may place a premium investment on eliminating conflict minerals in their supply chains. This allows medical device or automotive companies to take advantage of these efforts without bearing the full cost.

When it comes to how to incorporate sustainability into procurement options, most people gravitate to the obvious categories of packaging and transportation, which is a good starting point. However, there are numerous other areas to deliver robust savings to both the planet and bottom line. For example, with IT hardware, simple tactics such as increasing the duration between refresh cycles of laptops and mobile phones can help reduce toxic electronic waste.

Frequently, sustainable products and services are expensive due to lack of economies of scale. If procurement across major companies decides

---

[10] For more information on this program, please see Outland Denim 2020 Sustainability Report, https://cdn.shopify.com/s/files/1/0098/3669/1535/files/outland-denim-sustainability-report-2020-2.pdf?v=1596437271.

to collectively demand and/or invest in sustainable offerings, the collective will action those at a reasonable price. For example, companies have been steadily moving en masse to cloud-hosting solutions at a fairly rapid pace. The collective user base can demand, and more likely achieve, major cloud providers to operate sustainable data centers—powered by locally sourced renewable energy, energy-efficient servers/devices, and sustainability climate-controlled facilities.

2.7.4 Digital levers to achieve ESG goals

We have seen how supplier diversity, sustainability, and FL and CM may be key ESG goals. Your company may have others. Regardless of what your company's ESG goals are, my key message is that digital procurement has levers to accomplish these goals.

Requisitioning

An often-used adage, "We cannot achieve what we cannot measure," is particularly relevant here. The requisitioning system can be a great place to gain complete dynamic visibility of what is being bought, set annual targets, and closely track progress toward these sustainability goals. A well-designed requisition system will give users the ability to factor sustainability in their purchases. Specifically, when a user searches for an item and is given the available options, a good system will flag which is the sustainability choice (or any other ESG designation), replete with encouragement to ask them to make the right choice or even ask them why. That means every time a requisitioner makes a sustainable purchase, they will automatically contribute to a net-zero goal. If you imagine tens of thousands of requisitioners buying billions of dollars of goods and services, the ability for users to make a sustainable choice can make a meaningful change to a sustainability score—without any direct intervention from procurement. Software solutions are starting to provide this functionality as the default (see figure 15 on page 92).

Furthermore, if users are serially not making sustainable choices, then procurement can intervene to figure out why and fix the problem, whether it's user awareness or an issue in the system. For example, an even better-designed requisition system would be programmed to intelligently make the green choice before offering up the options to the user. That way the cost–benefit trade-off is done across the entire spend without the business user

Figure 15
ESG requisitioning example

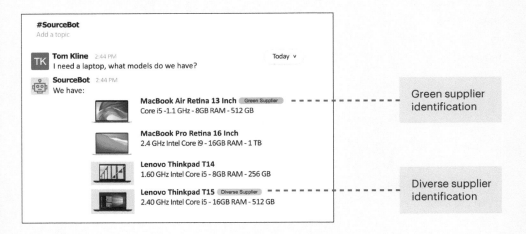

Source: Kearney analysis

ever being aware of it. Conceivably, one could imagine a scenario in which 100 percent of spend—in certain categories at least—could be from green suppliers at the same cost or even less without users ever being any the wiser that they were contributing to the greater green good. It's important to recognize and reward buyers who make consistent green choices and contribute toward the enterprise goals; this can be a tool to drive the right behavior. One could even include gamification and leaderboards to spur competition toward driving better outcomes.

Part of an effective procurement operation is procurement's ability to effectively understand its supply base. When it comes to sustainability, having visibility to all suppliers' capabilities, not just the tier 1 strategic ones, is crucial. In years past, lack of information transparency made this goal nearly unachievable. But now the data foundation discussed above makes this information ubiquitous. These networks enable buyers to include sustainability requirements in sourcing events and as the co-efficient for complex sourcing events as in the diverse supplier examples above. This information can also be used as a vital input in the supplier relationship management capability for balanced scorecards across all segments of suppliers.

Digitization

On a tactical level, the simple act of moving from paper invoices to a fully digitized payment process will automatically reduce paper and ink use, and lower the carbon footprint from traditional mail delivery. Every digitization effort can be quantified as generating tangible progress toward the net-zero goal.

Sourcing

As we have seen, good sourcing measures risk. Risk mitigation/potential can be factored into the awards so as to not overcommit to a particular supplier in a particular region. Similarly, good sourcing can accomplish ESG objectives such as supplier diversity or sustainability.

Every sourcing event can factor sustainability metrics into the various award options. That way, every award of business has a tangible sustainability benefit. The benefits could be as simple as compostable packaging or carbon-neutral delivery vehicles. You can also reduce carbon by sourcing green electricity, or through a vast array of green choices within facilities management (cleaners, light bulbs, HVAC). Each of these benefits can meaningfully contribute to ESG objectives.

Furthermore, there are going to be specific opportunities such as value engineering to design more sustainability into products. As several of our clients have done, this could be working to find innovative solutions to waste management. Instead of simply finding suppliers to haul waste away, savvy procurement people have engaged with different suppliers to break down the waste and sell it for alternative sources. Or by employing a combination of robotics, automation, and intelligent systems, companies can improve the reuse of disposable packaging and components.

Finally, as 3D printing matures, there will be opportunities for procurement to engage 3D printing capabilities for certain categories. Currently some MRO items such as masks, tools, nuts, bolts, or clamps can be printed. This means that for every printed item there is a benefit to be calculated for the manufacturing, packaging, and delivery environmental impact avoidance.

Next level

Several years ago, we did a prototype simulation project for a wind farm provider. We modeled dynamic simulation and "what-if" optimization of turbine service scheduling and crew planning. This example, while an operations problem, demonstrates the power of visually simulating cost trade-offs, a skill next-generation procurement folks need to have and should be using today. The goal was to evaluate different behaviors that factored in daily revenue per turbine, service crew costs, turbine replacement costs, repair costs, and service costs. The goal was to maximize profit by optimizing service crew utilization with an optimal repair plan that extended the life of each individual turbine. With this type of analytics we were able to easily maximize profitability per unit while reducing maintenance costs. However, it would be easy to extend the model to incorporate sustainability into the maintenance side of the equation if we mapped the as-is maintenance scheduling and deployments and calculated the baseline carbon footprint. Then in the scenario planning we could model for sustainability improvement by either changing the types of vehicle, shortening routes, or achieving other efficiency gains. Therefore, any recommended changes would contribute to the net-zero goal (see figure 16).

Simulations and analytical models can be a great way to understand the long-term true impact of business/sourcing decisions. As mentioned earlier, moving the needle on sustainability may not happen within a few months or even years. Our ability to model sourcing decisions with variables to quantify the impact of sustainable choices in the long term can be very powerful, especially when evaluating trade-offs.

Running the meter

If procurement wants to add value in the digital era, it needs to think entrepre-neurially. (I realize that sounds about as clichéd as a consultant can sound.) My point is that entrepreneurs are risk takers, usually high-risk, high-reward types. CPOs have the opportunity at this moment to be entrepreneurs. You can bet big and get high returns. You can commit to achieving 50 percent of the sustainability goal or awarding 50 percent of your business to diverse suppliers. You can sign up for strong year-on-year cost savings. Not only is it the right thing to do, but it is also achievable with the use of good digital tools.

Figure 16
Dynamic wind farm simulation

Operational availability

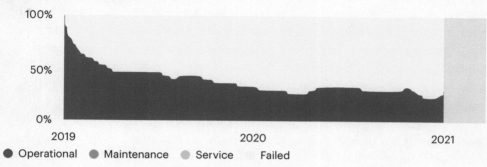

Operational utilization

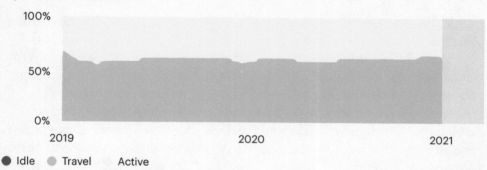

Revenue and expenses

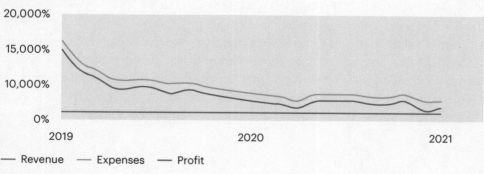

Source: Kearney analysis

You can simply set up a meter with three dials: cost, sustainability, and diversity. As each sourcing award is made, each requisition made, and each cost savings generated, each individual meter will run. Imagine: every time a diverse supplier is awarded business, the meter ticks forward. Every time a user makes a green choice, the meter runs. You could even add a fourth dial that calculates opportunity cost. This will show the progress that could have been and gives the leadership and the diversity officer the ability to undertake direct programs to change behavior. Furthermore, you could embed clever gamification where users achieve various statuses (for example, advocate, difference maker, rising star, superstar). Studies have proven that award labels will spur behavior in particular directions.[11] Taking this further, companies could reward this behavior with public acknowledgement and/or monetary rewards (or, ideally, donations).

2.7.5 What are we buying?

Product design, a topic worthy of its own book, has the potential to affect the entire life cycle of a product. For example, design can dictate the materials used to build the product and make way for innovative end-of-life solutions to reduce waste going to landfill. Procurement should play the role of a strategic partner for R&D with design teams helping ensure "pragmatic" design concepts become reality at an accelerated pace. Procurement can find or develop the right suppliers to provide materials for these sustainability-driven designs. This could be proactively working to find innovative solutions to waste management. Benefits can range from savings on paying to haul waste product away or breaking it down and using it for alternative sources of consumption.

2.8 Active risk through digital means

Any risk is signaled ahead of time. Systems that respond well to risks have often identified and acted upon those signals ahead of time. Systems that respond poorly to risks often claim that the risks were unimaginable. For example, in the shock after the tragedy of September 11, 2001, some pundits claimed that nobody could have imagined that terrorists would take a 747

---

[11] Anderson, Ashton & Huttenlocher, Daniel & Kleinberg, Jon & Leskovec, June 2013, "Steering user behavior with badges," Proceedings of the 22nd International Conference on World Wide Web, 95-106

plane and use it as a flying bomb. Other pundits pointed to a Tom Clancy novel and an attempted 1974 hijacking at Baltimore/Washington International Airport. The signals were out there and people weren't paying attention. This is the danger of trusting humans with signal identification and action.

Today, signals should be telling us about risks in the technology that underpins our entire global digital infrastructure. The Internet backbone, individual computers, IoT devices, and just about everything else that is connected is largely insecure. When you talk to security people, you realize how fragile and susceptible digital systems are to breach.

Obviously, this has huge implications for supply chains in terms of track-and-trace/providence, the people who operate supply chains, and suppliers. No matter how much technology you throw at security, the real problem is people. For example, crypto-locker viruses are malware that gets installed where unsuspecting users click on malicious emails that infects their computers and locks them out of their computer unless they pay a ransom. Most high-profile security breaches (The Home Depot, Best Buy, Target) originate from suppliers' systems. And what gets sourced, manufactured, and delivered is susceptible to human subterfuge (and no, blockchain will not solve this).

So once we have new ERP systems, we'll need new forms of digital security. It's premature to delve into specifics at this early stage of evolution, because the area will soon be transformed by massive new thinking, development, and imagination, but it's important to understand the need to stay abreast of these developments in the context of our supply base.

2.8.1 Framework for active risk

We have sacrificed risk, ESG, and innovation to drive cost savings. We have over-indexed on cost savings by a huge margin. That's how we found ourselves off-balance and collectively unable to respond to the pandemic. Whatever risk models and tools we had were woefully inadequate and very much event-based. They lacked the necessary precision and noise cancellation.

The problem with event-based tools is that they're imprecise and generally overwhelm the users with useless notifications. In response, users usually turn off said notifications. Moreover, when risk signals have been generated the natural response has been to fire off a survey to suppliers. This puts an additional burden on the supplier, which is likely trying to address the crisis at hand. And if the supplier has multiple customers then that supplier is potentially spending as much time responding to the crisis as they are responding to the onslaught of surveys and phone calls. Once we get the information back from the supply base, pair that with the risk signals and taking action is often poorly executed and most assuredly labor intensive.

There is a much better way. This is where *active risk management* shines. We should be able to take vast swaths of external risk signals (for example, financial, cyber, events, social, geographic, news, and ESG), combine those with internal operational data (for example, bills of materials, lead times, forecast, and inventory) and data on supplier capacity/resiliency/capability, teach the machine to process all this information, and distill it down into a usable data set. From there, we humans can apply strategy, or even system-suggested strategic choices, to determine the relevant steps to ameliorate the impact of a given risk. Here we can make the necessary trade-offs to reallocate supply, add new supply, or simply absorb the impact. Then we can take the relevant action by hand or let the machine do it. The key is that we track recommendations the system made and whether the human took the relevant action. This will do two things: first, it will help the machine learn the correct response to events, and secondly it will ensure that the humans are taking the appropriate and timely actions.

I call this approach *signal, strategy, action* (SSA) (see figure 17). This illustration highlights the power of the SSA framework. The left column automates the collection of the vast amount of data signals. There are more data signals coming into any enterprise function than humans can review. Hence it is necessary. We can teach the machine over time to ingest this vast number of signals and process them down to what's relevant and needs human evaluation. This discrete set of information requires us to apply business objectives and strategy to the relevant external signals. While this is best done by a human, there can still be machine augmentation to help formulate the different scenarios and trade-offs. From there we can create a list of recommended actions that can be executed either by human or by machine.

Figure 17
Signal, strategy, action

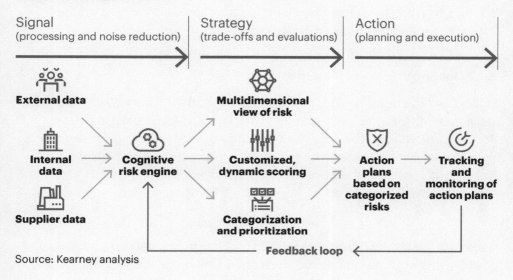

Signal
(processing and noise reduction)

Strategy
(trade-offs and evaluations)

Action
(planning and execution)

External data

Internal data

Supplier data

Cognitive risk engine

Multidimensional view of risk

Customized, dynamic scoring

Categorization and prioritization

Action plans based on categorized risks

Tracking and monitoring of action plans

Feedback loop

Source: Kearney analysis

The SSA framework can be seen in the real world through a real-world example. Let's say there's a hurricane headed toward Puerto Rico. There's going to be a series of continually updated external signals tracking the predicted location, severity, and impact of the hurricane. Those signals need to be matched up with internal product data that identifies which product lines and suppliers are likely to be hit and those that could be hit if the hurricane is worse than predicted. All this input can be processed; again, the more we teach the machine how to interpret hurricane data and the potential disruptive impact, the smarter we can make the signaling output. The signaling output should give us a clear indication of how much of a particular product is at risk for either supply or production disruption. From here we can decide what strategic choices we have available to us. Do we contract for higher priced commodities to ensure continuity of supply? If so, how long will delivery to the affected area take? Do we release safety stock? Can we make adjustments to other product lines? How long will any of these changes take? Once we make these decisions, we will then have a series of recommended actions to take such as finding alternative supply sources, querying the manufacturers on whether production lines can be switched, or executing the movement of safety stock.

2.8.2 Guiding principles for active risk

Active risk requires a completely new approach to third party/supplier risk management. This is not an incremental fix. First and foremost, we need to *stop the survey*! As discussed in Section 1.2, endlessly surveying your suppliers on the latest potential risk to hit the news is a lazy and incomplete way to measure risk. Integration between supply chain systems and various systems from outsourced manufacturing suppliers will eliminate a series of questions used in surveys.

Moreover, the aforementioned analytics that model risk vector, supplier location, and potential impact will further eliminate the need for the survey because we will dynamically have access to the core information we need to make risk-based decisions in real time.

As part of our new risk management approach, we need our category and commodity managers to be enabled to model different strategies in response to various risk situations. Part of their job descriptions should include doing forward-looking what-if analyses to test and create alternative outcomes in case of disruption. Then as the risks unfold, the proper strategy can be quickly deployed based on changing dynamics. The strategy should then be matched with clear roles and responsibilities in the response and finding the right balance between cost and risk mitigation/resilience. It is important to include accountability measures that continually track and evaluate the efficacy of strategy and actioning. Companies need to continually test the efficacy to ensure the proper allocation of resources in response to crises. Finally, automation should do the heavy lifting on low-risk events and should augment human intelligence augmentation on higher-risk events. Automation can also help run simulations and do the forward-looking scenario planning. This automation should take the form of anticipatory solutions that prompt users to think about what threats could happen and how to respond, and predictive solutions that predict threats that will likely happen (see sidebar: A real-world active risk story).

A real-world active risk story

Banjo is a small analytics/AI company based in Utah. It was founded in 2010 by Damien Patton. Using approximately $125 million in venture-capital funding, including a large portion from Softbank, it seeks to revolutionize the flow of information to first responders. Its flagship product Live Time uses AI to process, interpret, and inform first responders to live situations as they are unfolding. The AI ingests real-time social media, traffic, weather, and video feeds to give first responders timely and hopefully more accurate information. Banjo very clearly states that all personal identifying information (PII) is stripped from its data collection and analysis. It promises to transform law enforcement by providing the panacea of faster, more accurate information. Obviously, this can be a boost for active shooter situations, kidnappings, riots, and other such activities where seconds and minutes make the difference between life and death.

Seeing the potential of this technology, the state of Utah signed a near-to $21 million contract with Banjo. According to OneZero, the State of Utah gave Banjo access to all data from Utah Department of Transportation video cameras and data from the Utah Department of Public Safety and Highway Patrol. The scope included all Utah counties, cities, and universities.[12]

The story so far would have been simply a small but interesting development in the use of AI for policing. But then it was revealed that Patton as a young man belonged to the Ku Klux Klan. Not only had he been a member but he also testified under oath that he participated in a drive-by shooting at a Tennessee synagogue. Naturally the state of Utah immediately suspended its contract with Banjo while it conducted an independent review of the situation. The Utah Attorney General's office issued a statement noting that they were "shocked and dismayed at reports that Banjo's founder had any affiliation with any hate group or groups in his youth. Neither the AG office nor anyone in the AG's office was aware of these affiliations or actions. They are indefensible. He has said so himself."

(continued on next page)

---

[12] Dave Gershgorn, "Banjo CEO Resigns Following Revelation of KKK Ties,"OneZero, May 11, 2020, https://onezero.medium.com/banjo-ceo-resigns-following-revelation-of-kkk-ties-6a2152d8cc35

A real-world active risk story (continued)

From an SRM perspective, this situation was an unmitigated disaster. It demonstrated the tremendous weakness in the State of Utah's SRM strategy (if one even exists).

But the story should also serve as a warning to any company or entity that is contracting for AI services or technology. AI is highly susceptible to the biases of its creators. Consider that to operate a successful algorithm you must train it with a significant set of training data. If the training data contains biases then the algorithms will inherently display biased behavior. For example, if you scan 100 million news and journal articles you'll find that the term "black sheep" occurs more frequently than "white sheep" by a margin of about 25:1. Therefore the AI would conclude by mathematic formula that the color of sheep is black. So despite Banjo's claim that it's not sending PII to first responders, it's quite possible that its algorithm easily (if only accidentally) introduces bias to the responding units. Perhaps police officers get twitchier, show up guns drawn. Perhaps ambulances hold back, take their time. In short, introducing this bias puts marginalized populations at greater risk.

Therefore, any supplier, working on behalf of a government entity, that consumes data from citizens, interrogates it, and provides it to emergency services personnel should be treated as a tier 1 supplier. That means these suppliers should be thoroughly vetted and monitored.

This is where good supplier intelligence tools come into play. The same AI tools operated by Banjo are used by supplier intelligence tools. In the digital era, you don't have to be Sherlock Holmes stitching together random pieces of information to solve the unsolvable—all you have to do is look. Sometimes all you need to do is light Googling.

2.9 Putting the R back in SRM

Historically, the "best practice" has been to segment suppliers based on importance to the business. Traditional thinking states that if you have 10,000 suppliers then that is far too many to manage directly. To address this problem, we segment suppliers into tiers. Tier 1 suppliers (~10 percent) represent the most crucial to our ability to operate and have high interactions with the business, whereas tier 4 (~60–70 percent) suppliers are non-strategic and only have transactional interactions with the business. The level of connectedness between business and supplier is correlated to tiering. For example, a tier 1 supplier for a CPG manufacturer might be one who provides the main ingredients for the product—it would get an elevated amount of attention compared to the office supplies supplier who would be a tier 4.

However, COVID-19 just exposed the limitations of this approach. The ability to operate those manufacturing lines is dependent on having janitorial supplies and services. If you can't provide soap and basic sanitation, then you cannot operate the facility. When a pandemic breaks out, soap and janitorial services become a primary commodity and provide an impediment to business operations. How many risk models looked at janitorial supplies?

Another example was videoconferencing software. This was treated as a nice-to-have instead of a crucial need. However, almost overnight video conferencing software was put to the test. Zoom quickly became mission-critical for companies, governments, schools, and community groups. Before 2020, how many companies treated this as a business must-have?

A more fundamental question we rarely answer is whether 10,000 suppliers is the right number. We've learned from COVID-19 that we need a greater starting level of insight and control over the supply base and it needs to be fluid, especially for indirect spend.

When the focus was cost savings, non-tier 1 suppliers were treated as non-strategic. The problem comes when you enter a crisis and you need to know if your suppliers can give you what you need, whether they're sustaining the crisis, and whether they can help you. If you throttled them for a few nickels right before the crisis, they may not be willing to help out much.

2.9.1 What's needed in SRM software

At its core, SRM is about managing supplier behavior to drive value. That value is derived from business strategy. Good SRM capabilities are made up of the components shown in figure 18.

No system performs all these functions. It would be impossible for a single provider to deliver all these capabilities and achieve the necessary quality. Any provider that claims to do so is lying. Each one of these components could be its own suite of individual capabilities/insights. In the era of APIs, when integration can be done with seven lines of code, there's no reason to build all these components with a single provider. The best approach is to find the *single pane of glass* that provides all these integration points. Also, this approach avoids the big-bang approach and allows for an agile onboarding of capabilities while minimizing risk.

All this information enables category managers to have all the data they need at their fingertips. With that information, not only can they effectively and efficiently manage their category but they can also start to do the proactive modeling around should-cost and scenario planning to effectively manage risk. Most category managers struggle to get a fraction of the data enumerated above and spend weeks chasing it down. But as that information is seamlessly bubbled up, two important things happen. First, category managers can cover more categories. Second, the automation that underpins this information transparency means that automated action can be taken. Instead of doing a single sourcing event once a year because that's what the plan is resourced for, with automation you can continuously monitor the signals and put work out to bid as market conditions fluctuate (see sidebar on page 106: Customer relationship management versus supplier relationship management maturity).

Figure 18
Key SRM technology capabilities

Functionality	Market maturity	Description
Information management	High	Onboarding, collection, and maintenance of supplier information (including harmonization and enrichment)
Identification	Medium	Easily search and select new and existing suppliers in any tool
Relationship management	Medium	Manage all interactions with suppliers and orchestrate development, fitness, and joint process improvement programs
Risk management	High	Evaluate holistic risk (e.g., financial, security, event, cyber, etc.) across all supplier tiers
Corporate responsibility	High	Track and achieve corporate responsibility targets (e.g., sustainability, diversity, forced labor avoidance)
Segmentation	Low	Develop supplier tiering map and identify alternative options, if needed
Performance management	Medium	Monitor supplier performance against qualitative and quantitative measures
Collaboration	Medium	Innovate with suppliers and solicit/exchange ideas
Benchmarks/ pricing	Medium	Compare price competitiveness
Transactional	Medium	Invoicing, PO management, payments

Source: Kearney analysis

Customer relationship management versus supplier relationship management maturity

Perhaps the hardest dynamic to reconcile is how sophisticated customer relationship management (CRM) can be, and how immature SRM is. CRM feels like it's light years ahead of SRM. Granted, CRM methodology has been around a lot longer—dating back to Rolodex cards. Additionally, CRM got a huge boost in the salesforce automation efforts that Salesforce.com pioneered over the past two decades, whereas SRM is a relatively new phenomenon. But still the two couldn't be any more different in terms of maturity and adoption. It's thus useful to deconstruct CRM and SRM into their component pieces.

In CRM, the goal is to manage potential and current customers (sometimes called accounts). To do that we need to ascertain who the people we know are and what their contact information is. From there, we need to track every interaction with them.

If they are a prospect:

— Do they know us?

— Have we sent them information, did they click on it, did they unsubscribe, did they forward it?

— Have we done a demo or multiple demos?

— Are we in front of the decision-maker?

— Did they invite us to an RFP? Did we win?

— Are we negotiating?

— Are we discussing terms and conditions?

If they are a customer:

— How big is the account?

— Are we doing quarterly business reviews (QBRs), top-to-tops (meetings between the top executives of two companies to strengthen an existing relationship)?

— How many opportunities are we invited to; how many are we winning?

— Are we sending outbound (upsell) marketing information, did they click on it, did they unsubscribe, did they forward it?

— Are we inviting them to our events?

— Are we doing joint press releases?

— Who do we know beyond our current clients?

As procurement people, perhaps we imagine that salespeople, like us, just make it up as they go along with Excel spreadsheets. But the technology has evolved to support and often automate these steps. This is what we need to see in SRM as well (see Section 2.9).

Section III
How to do digital procurement

3.1 Learn and plan

The previous section laid out a bold new digital vision for procurement: an extensible ecosystem of very precise capabilities. This approach allows for a greater level of maturity and oversight while eliminating excuses. There's no longer a good excuse for having poor data quality, spend visibility, or inability to make cost savings. This vision will make things easier for business users and encourage value-creating behaviors without direct intervention. That applies to the transition as well. If you have to train people, you're doing digital wrong. If your rollout is measured in months or years, you're doing digital wrong. If your benefits are measured in months or years, you're doing it wrong.

This section will discuss how to make the journey to digital. We'll look at what it means to operate in an agile manner (for example, moving away from RFPs to MVPs). How to best engage IT so they participate in the journey instead of blocking it. We'll answer the question as to whether this is real or not. Digital done well will disrupt our existing operating models so we will cover the implications of this. Finally, we'll talk about where digital procurement goes next.

3.2 Starting the journey

Companies that don't have any procurement technology—those that are starting with a blank sheet of paper—are in the best position to achieve procurement excellence. These companies are not encumbered by poor-performing and costly legacy technology investments. They can simply leapfrog into the future. As this book has emphasized so far, we're no longer in the era of a single closed-loop system—that approach failed spectacularly over the past 20 years. Any vendor or consultant who tries to sell you a single end-to-end system is selling you an almost-guaranteed technical failure. Instead, building a digital procurement capability that works for the business (instead of hindering it) requires layering different levels of capability on top of one another.

3.2.1 Phase 0: The foundation

Your foundational capability should be a **P2P system**, which will provide a clear and concise way to manage spend. This includes setting up the various buying channels, invoicing, payments, and so forth. By streamlining this set of capabilities, you can put governance and control over the conduct of external expenditures. P2P includes payment terms, fraud prevention, buying with preferred providers, and so on. Moreover, this strong foundation will enable more advanced capabilities in other phases.

Additionally, companies should build a **data lake** capability. This is the ability to land all internal data and piped-in external data in a single (conceptual) container. The data lake allows you to create basic analytics in your early phase and more complex analytics in later phases. The data lake can be built in-house with IT resources using popular cloud platforms.

Once the data lake is built, then the first order of business is to construct a robust **spend cube**. You can do this using one of the many sophisticated spend tools in the market. Depending on how many suppliers you're using, you may also benefit from implementing a data foundation, which will help keep the data lake and spend visibility tool accurate and up to date at scale.

3.2.2 Phase 1: Creating value and maturity

In this phase the goal is to onboard **sourcing** and **contracting** capabilities. The sourcing capabilities will give immediate value by bringing greater supply and demand leverage. Ideally, you will onboard both simple and advanced sourcing (expressive bidding) capabilities, depending on the types of categories and the spend volume. Depending on sourcing volume, categories, and opportunity assessment, it might be useful to have access to robust market intelligence tools as well.

For contracting, the most important goal is to get negotiated contracts into a singular (or at least logical) document repository. On top of that, plug-in contract analytics capabilities will extract all the relevant information in the contracts and provide the necessary insights to inform sourcing and P2P activities. It's worth doing e-signature where governmental regulations allow it. Capabilities such as contract authoring, templating, and workflows will come in later phases.

3.2.3 Phase 2: Going further on value

In this phase the goal is to expand sourcing and contracting capabilities and—depending on the industry—to have greater integration with planning and new product introduction related tools. For **sourcing**, this phase is an opportunity to employ solutions to automate three bids and a buy for tail and low threshold sourcing. Similarly, you can use tools to automate advanced sourcing activities. In parallel, employing a series of category-specific self-service solutions can unlock significant value. Examples include consulting, marketing, print (legal), travel, facilities management, and temp labor.

At this point it's appropriate to onboard more robust **contracting** capabilities such as contract authoring, templating, and workflows. While these capabilities are important and look great on paper, they're time-consuming and expensive to implement. Also, this is an area with significant dependence on the legal department, so these initiatives can get bogged down in minutiae. Many companies have impaled themselves while chasing the elusive concept of contract management excellence. Example tools in this area are iCertis and Apptus.

3.2.4 Phase 3: Operating in the 21st century

If you make it to this phase, congratulations—you're in an exclusive group of leaders. You have moved from "spend management" to "value creation." Here is where you can take all the capabilities from the previous phases and upskill (automated) category/commodity management capabilities on top of the overall procurement function. You have the ability to create forward-looking insights, do scenario modeling, and work proactively. Specifically, the previous investments should enable you to perform advanced SRM, risk, ESG, and innovation initiatives.

3.2.5 Wait, phases 0–3 look oddly familiar...

To some degree the approach above is reductive; just a lighter, risk-mitigated, and cost-effective version of the traditional approach. It's a reflection of the fact that the complexity of operating in today's enterprises forces some level of standardization. However, if we looked at value creation as the primary driver, the entire equation would change. Hypothetically, and generously, let's imagine the scenario benefit of a P2P system is $30–40 million over five years and it actually gets delivered for a cost of $20 million (I know; a huge leap of the imagination). By contrast, I can run a single-sourcing optimization event for the transportation category and save $100 million that will get realized in a month or two for roughly $200,000 of expenses. Why wouldn't we simply get some sourcing tools to accelerate those efforts and then adopt other capabilities over time? This is the dichotomy and tension between S2C activities and P2P activities. It's easy to garner a lot of wins with S2C activities through the bevy of nuanced sourcing tools such as basic sourcing, tail spend automation, sourcing optimization, services sourcing, and category-specific solutions. But, operationalizing those savings requires P2P. Striking that balance is the trick. You must not sublimate the power of S2C simply to placate the rigidity of P2P. Conversely, S2C cannot be a wild free-for-all disconnected from the transactional control of the P2P system. This is why the ecosystem approach is so necessary in the short term. Longer term, once open exchanges and smart contracts come to maturity, it will open the throttle for S2C activities.

3.3 MVP factory: stop doing RFPs and start doing MVPs

The era of the seven-figure procurement software deal is over. As the *ecosystem* comes to fruition, the way we buy software will become much more flexible. We must stop doing *requests for proposals* (RFPs) and start doing *minimum viable products* (MVPs). MVPs originate in the *agile* software world where the goal is to build a continuous and early feedback loop to product development. This enables developers to make timely adjustments to maximize user satisfaction without waiting for the product to be near completion before getting solid user feedback. Before the *agile* methodology, the *waterfall* was the traditional method of software development. This approach put significant effort up front soliciting requirements from users, followed by the developers going away to write code and then coming back toward the end of the development cycle with a largely complete tool to solicit user feedback. Naturally, this turned out be a suboptimal way of developing software that frustrated both users and developers (with lots of finger-pointing). Unsurprisingly, system integrations have followed a similar *waterfall* paradigm: long software requirements gathering efforts, then running lengthy RFPs, followed by an even longer evaluation period, followed by a selection, and then implementation.

The *waterfall* approach to systems integration has left users wanting, and more importantly left CPOs wondering how and why their benefits never materialized. We need to move to a more *agile* way of systems integration. It's no longer about soliciting bids from a fixed set of vendors but rather identifying crucial capabilities that the business needs—because it's different for every industry—and then scouting and evaluating solutions in a hands-on manner. We should no longer be simply looking at analyst reports to determine what others say. We should build our own comprehensive fact base using our evaluations, experiences, and stories from others we trust. Then, once we identify the requisite solutions, we adopt them in an MVP style approach, where we try the tool out over the course of three to four weeks (or less). If it works, then we formally adopt it; if it doesn't then we abandon the effort. This keeps costs constrained, resources optimized, and foregrounds the time to value. If a particular effort takes more than six weeks you are doing *agile* wrong.

Staring at 10, 20, or 30 start-ups can be a bit overwhelming. Or, more accurately, being inundated every day with a new start-up promising to deliver millions of dollars of savings through the use of "AI," "Blockchain," or some other nonsense is exhausting. At the same time, there are companies that are building truly innovative solutions. The question becomes, how to weed through all the noise to build an effective plan?

The best way to frame this is to set up an MVP factory (see figure 19 on page 114). As the figure shows, the factory should serve as a funnel. The wide end continually monitors the market for new solutions. How does one monitor and find out about all these new solutions? My suggestion is to follow a few influencers on LinkedIn, talk to peers, and set up a cadence of engaging with solution providers. One innovation I expect to see is a new type of organization that monitors and evaluates new technology but that importantly is not funded by the vendors. These soon-to-be organizations will provide a more robust and less biased view on the market than we have seen before. In other words, as technology solution providers have matured, one of the ancillary innovations will be new organizations (public and private) that evaluate them.

Figure 19
MVP (minimum viable product) factory

MVP shortlist

MVP 1

A Business need and impact

B Data

C Enablement strategy

D Feasibility availability

Readiness checklist

Team

— Who's the category lead?
— Who's the data lead?
— What level of involvement is required?
— What other SMEs are needed?

Data

— Where's the data?
— How can the data be accessed?
— What are the dependencies?

Tech

— What platform(s) are required?
— What is the time/complexity to procure/onboard new platform(s)?

Value case and scoping

— Expected benefits range?
— Metrics to track progress?
— Stakeholders aligned on scope?

MVP

Source: Kearney analysis

As the list of potential solutions grows, it should be continually evaluated against what will create value across efficiency, effectiveness, and experience dimensions. There's a simple way to think about this: if you had $1 million to try out five start-ups, which would you choose and why? This is a helpful way to simplify. For every 10 solutions evaluated, expect to pilot three to five to make it to the pilot stage. The key to running a successful pilot is to clearly define your objectives and success criteria and limit your scope. Obviously, the business needs to be engaged. This means finding people in the business willing to go on what will be a bumpy but rewarding ride. For example, any category manager who spends a large portion of their time chasing data and manipulating it in Excel might be very motivated to pilot and embrace new solutions. Getting cooperation from IT is also crucial. Their remit is going to be slightly different so it's important to convey to them, in the strongest possible terms, the business value that will be projected from this capability. No IT person wants to stand in the way of millions in potential savings and operational efficiency. Forward-looking IT people will not be afraid of this and in many cases will be able to help and contribute. For instance, most IT groups have data lakes and they're often willing to incorporate procurement's needs into what they have. So it's more a matter of communicating needs and speaking their language than anything else (see Section 3.4 on talking to the CIO).

By nature, pilots are trials. A large number of failures should be expected. Every failure is a huge learning experience. Ultimately the MVP process is about building comfort and capability with these new digital technologies, and getting the necessary resources involved. Successful pilots then move toward a formal onboarding process. A good success rate is onboarding one or two out of the 10 that made it to the evaluation phase.

Formally, the process can be broken into four types of activity: watch, engage, pilot, and scale. First, we must continually scan the market for innovations that improve or disrupt what we're doing. Next, we must engage with potential solution providers to understand what they can do today and what they're willing to do tomorrow. It's important to note that this may include engaging academics, entrepreneurs, venture capitalists, industry organizations, and other nontraditional sources. Then we must pilot solutions in an agile way. Again, three to six weeks top to figure out if a particular solution is going to work. Finally, we need to be able to scale in a measured and mindful way. This process should always be accretive to existing operations and never disruptive (see sidebar on page 116: All about start-ups).

All about start-ups

Start-ups are all over the procurement space. As we have discussed, this is because both innovators and venture capitalists see procurement as strategically very important, while being wildly underserved by technology. So your journey toward procurement excellence will surely involve interacting with start-ups. Here are some tips on how to think about those relationships.

Silicon Valley immersion sessions

In November 2017 we were invited to speak to a CPO's leadership team. In advance of that we co-created our first Future of Procurement whitepaper with the CPO. We worked with him to chart the digitally enabled future course of procurement for his organization and for us more broadly in the market. We had a lot of momentum going into that workshop. However, once we walked into the room it was clear the client had soured on technology's ability to deliver the desired end state. We probed a little more and found out that the CPO and his head of technology had just returned a few weeks earlier from a trip to Silicon Valley to do a meet-and-greet hosted by one of our competitors. The goal of this session was to introduce bank executives to fintechs. The meeting was a disaster for our client, who came away with the feeling that technology would never get there. Sensing an opportunity, I threw down the gauntlet and said that next time he came to the Bay Area I would arrange a highly cultivated start-up immersion session. In March 2018 he took me up on the offer, and with only three weeks to pull it together, we did a one-day immersion session that was a stellar success. This became the genesis of our hugely successful Silicon Valley immersion sessions where we invite CPOs to come to San Francisco for two days to meet founders of start-ups. I curate who comes and give a rationale behind why each is there. Before the session I take two crucial actions. First, I talk to the start-ups and guide them on how to have a successful session. Second, I communicate to the CPOs who is coming and why I picked them.

Evaluating start-ups

When evaluating start-ups, it's useful to categorize them across four tiers of increasing maturity. Tier 1 start-ups have an initial product, some initial seed funding, and a handful of clients. Tier 2 start-ups have some funding such as series A or B and a couple dozen clients. Tier 3 start-ups have a ton of funding (series C or D) and a significant and growing client base. Naturally these lines are arbitrary and individual companies can quickly and fluidly move across them (in both directions).

Savvy executives engage with tier 1 and tier 2 start-ups because it affords them the opportunity to influence product direction. However, the trade-off is that there will be natural growing pains and so leaders will want to do pilots and segment work to limit risk. Here, prudent change management is vital. Tier 3 start-ups typically offer a great product, but their primary motivation is preparing for a transaction IPO (see figure 20 on page 118).

Further, to successfully engage these start-ups, CPOs need to connect directly with the founders. Otherwise it's too easy for the messaging to get lost in translation or buried under some underling's fear.

Concluding tips for start-ups

I have sat through a lot of technology pitches over the years. The most effective start-ups give a three-to-five-minute discussion of what they built and why and then jump into a demo that's targeted for the audience at hand and then can get into a discussion of *how to* with the audience. Unfortunately, most start-ups make the mistake of spending 25-35 minutes going through a PPT file explaining what they do, leaving precious little time for a demo and questions. Moreover, most start-ups struggle to effectively explain what they do, especially to an executive audience. My recommendation is that early-stage companies work with organizations or advisors who can help them with their positioning, presentation, and engagement. Trust me when I say that this issue is pervasive!

Figure 20
Start-up tiering

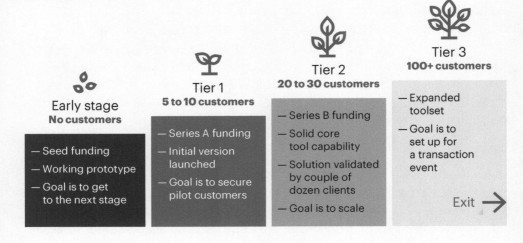

Source: Kearney analysis

3.4 Engaging with the CIO

Ideally, the procurement–IT relationship should be amicable, if not collaborative. There's no reason for it not to be. Unfortunately, often procurement is unable to effectively articulate its needs to IT. This leads to the inevitable communication and decision gap. Bridging this gap is one of the greatest keys to success in digital procurement. A strong CIO–CPO relationship will be mutually beneficial. This means CPOs and their teams have to be bridge-builders to CIOs, and their teams must be comfortable meeting their IT counterparts where they are. But under no circumstances should procurement cede its power to IT. If the CIO chooses to be recalcitrant, the CPO needs to be able to stand up to them and seek top-down intervention. With procurement the stakes are too high to simply acquiesce.

IT's knee-jerk response to technology initiatives often is, "What's the business value?" It's understandable that they ask the question—every technology initiative should have a value associated with it. But, when "business value" becomes an excuse for avoiding work, then there's an issue. Looking at the spider chart, nearly every label on that chart represents massive value. If each solution didn't deliver significant value, then they wouldn't exist. So when IT makes blanket assumptions that procurement technology initiatives are somehow not delivering value, they just look foolish. Moreover, if procurement can deliver $100 million of savings or more in a single year by employing a particular set of technologies, those initiatives should be high on the priority list and not given the excuse that "we don't have the resources"—best case it's an under-resourced IT function, worse case it's deliberate sandbagging. Entrepreneurially focused IT organizations are quick to realize that the group that owns the company's external spend can create significant value very quickly—indeed, the kind of value and visibility that makes its way to the corporate board, a win-win for both the CIO and CPO.

When it comes to choosing procurement technology, under no circumstances should procurement cede its decision-making authority to IT. That is legacy (if not lazy) thinking. When it comes to procurement systems, procurement is the stake owner and should demand (and articulate) what their requirements are.

To be fair, there are forward-thinking CIOs who understand and appreciate this dynamic. A few months before the pandemic broke out, I was giving a presentation of the material from this book and the CIO happened to be in the room. I took the opportunity to direct my comments at him just to see how he'd react. He was totally unfazed, and he doubled down on my messaging, saying that the technology was no big deal and that he would support procurement in whatever they wanted to do. But he challenged them to take ownership of what it means to operate in an agile manner (for example, how you onboard/offboard tools, evaluate them, and so on).

Often IT has made crucial technology investments that procurement is simply neither aware of nor taking advantage of. For example, nearly every IT organization invested in data lakes over the past decade. So when I ask why procurement doesn't have a data lake, the answer is usually *we have one, but procurement has never told us what they want in it or how they intend to govern it.* Perhaps the most useful starting point to engage with IT is to answer the question, "If I had a million dollars, where would I place my bets?" This is a great way to start a discussion about value and need (see sidebar on page 120: Is this a centralized or decentralized model?).

Is this a centralized or decentralized model?

When I talk to procurement people about these issues, some of them get nervous. "We're moving from a centralized to a decentralized model," they say, or sometimes it's vice versa. "What should we do?"

This is the wrong question. In a digital procurement environment, it doesn't matter whether you're centralized or decentralized. The future operating model will transcend procurement as we have known it. No longer will we debate centralized versus decentralized. Success will be measured by the ability to be nimble, operate efficiently, and expand influence over the business and the supply base. And these abilities will need to be executed by procurement functions that are smaller and tasked with varied strategic objectives.

In other words, one used to argue about whether the transactional purchasing gatekeeper was centralized or not, but now that argument is moot. That era is over. Those activities will be automated. They'll exist digitally, in a location that is both centralized and decentralized.

3.5 Is it real?

3.5.1 Author's note

I have been evangelizing about the future of procurement for nearly four years. In that time, I have witnessed an evolution from skepticism to curiosity to full-on embracing the digital reality. I have been persuasive enough to convert some of the skeptics. This started out with me in the role of enthusiastic cheerleader, to help push the function out of its collective stupor of mediocrity. The perspective was sufficiently interesting enough that it opened many conversations, presentations, and even hearts and minds. And then something curious happened around the beginning of 2020: digital rocketed to the top of most CPOs' agendas. Not source-to-pay, but truly transforming around digital and making this a top priority. This was before COVID-19, which accelerated the trend. Despite this, time and again I heard, "But is it real?" This made me pause and reflect because I didn't want to become guilty of what I was accusing the vendor–analyst–consultant community of: overselling something that wasn't achievable or realistic.

I decided I needed to prove beyond reasonable doubt that digital was real and transformative. So I reached out to technology providers that I felt were leading the way. I made two requests. First, I asked them to talk to their head of engineering/product so I could test whether they were truthful and able to deliver what they were proposing. I wanted to probe if what they called AI was truly cognitive versus machine learning, or simply decision tree logic, or (worse) something requiring manual intervention. My second request was to speak to a customer so I could ask how they were using the tool: did it match how the company was positioning it in the market, and (more importantly) what the effects were on their operating model? This is not a multiyear, longitudinal study to quantifiably prove a point. Instead, the goal here is to highlight the direction of travel by identifying what has been developed and validating that it both exists and is being used as advertised by clients. What follows are three examples.

3.5.2 LevaData

What the solution is supposed to do
LevaData is a direct sourcing tool. It's the epitome of the signal–strategy–action construct, which was a net innovation. According to the marketing material, the solution takes various internal and external signals, bounces them against a company's bills of materials, makes recommendations, and can take automatic action (for example, executing an RFP) based on the recommendation. Listening to the pitch one gets a very clear picture of what the future of direct sourcing will look like. It's easy to imagine plugging in risk, commodity pricing, and other inputs to make the solution robust and dynamic. The solution has deep roots in the high-tech space. Rajesh Kalidindi, the founder, comes from Cisco and created the solution, finding additional savings opportunities for what was believed to be commoditized categories. The simple premise is that instead of sourcing periodically at prescribed times (monthly, annually, whatever), LevaData creates a continuous view on the market so that sourcing can be undertaken at the moment an opportunity presents itself (for example, price fluctuation, demand increase, or risk signal).

What the solution can do

Undoubtedly the solution enables signal monitoring, smart matching to the BoM, and comes up with recommendations. For example, the intelligence engine will make recommendations to avoid shortages, balance supply and demand (and in future releases optimize), and provide options for risk avoidance. The ability to tie into upstream signals is still a bit bespoke (as opposed to plug-and-play). The part that will naturally follow in this evolution is the taking of autonomous action. This is the biggest leap to the future and after talking to the head of engineering I know they'll clearly get there, but it's a work in progress. Interestingly, during the client interview the interviewee pointed out that they believe LevaData will solve the remaining gaps and create a fully baked solution, but their real need is to have someone manage the strategic decisions.

How the client uses it

I interviewed two procurement people who work for a consumer electronics company. This is a company that like so many others moved to an external manufacturing model where more than 80 percent of the manufacturing is outsourced. A massive information gap ensued as the company lost visibility to BoM management. But the company still does commodity management because it can buy better than the CMs. When the contract manufacturing switch happened, it lost all its tier 2 commodity visibility.

This company was an early and eager adopter of LevaData. As with any company that is an early adopter, it experienced the expected ups and downs. In particular, it helped LevaData mature the client onboarding process. But it also netted the benefits. Today LevaData is the single source of truth for its direct spend and suppliers—something most companies long for. More importantly, when new products or existing product redesigns occur, it has all the costing information at its fingertips. The client's stakeholders leverage LevaData for pricing management: to accept pricing, autogenerate updates to pricing, and expand options. Their company has taken advantage of the automatic-accept pricing updates to create operational efficiencies by eliminating the *send me the Excel file* dynamic and creating a single source of truth. Perhaps the greatest benefit of being an early adopter (and reference client) is that it has a direct line to the leadership and can get any problems solved quickly.

From a change management point of view, the company's user base had high expectations (the magic button phenomenon) and a low tolerance for taking the journey. They had to explain the benefits, one user at a time, of using LevaData over spreadsheets. The moment commodity managers could see how to hit their goals, they saw it as a useful tool. What remains for them is to do more change management with their suppliers, taking ownership of the BoMs from the CMs, and to take advantage of LevaData's Smart RFX technology and New Product Introduction (NPI) capabilities. Their first attempt at the Smart RFX was rough and adoption was painful. However, they have subsequently scaled their supplier collaboration successfully with an improved change management capability. This customer uses Resilinc as well and they communicated that the data handoff between the two companies, at the time of the interview, was not where they had hoped, so definitely a growth area.

This company has experienced productivity improvements in the speed at which it receives bids and how those bids form the foundation for the negotiation plan. It's on a path to include market intelligence to forecasted recommendations, raw material trends, and pricing. The company is an active champion of LevaData, if not a pioneer, and is ready to roll out new features as they become available.

3.5.3 Fairmarkit

What the solution is supposed to do
Fairmarkit is an automated tail-spend solution. It will take inbound requisitions under a certain threshold and with a preapproved supply base and automatically put them out to market. In other words, an automated three bids and a buy on your core tail spend. Essentially, when a client gets mature enough with Fairmarkit, the tail spend manages itself.

What the solution can do
Having talked to Fairmarkit engineers, it's clear that their strength lies in their ability to make deep, complex integrations look easy. This is not a surprise given that a key value proposition is to be able to seamlessly plug straight into the requisition process, take data for the sourcing event, and put it back into the original requisition. If they didn't solve this then their company wouldn't survive their first client.

How the client uses it

Fairmarkit had me interview the CPO of a media company customer. The CPO became an earlier believer in the product, seeing it as a nimble and agile disruptor. He had the requirement that everything must be self-funding, though he was willing to re-engineer the business processes to take advantage of Fairmarkit's solution. For him, Fairmarkit systematically eliminated touch points in the procurement value chain. More shockingly, when he started there were a lot of high-level management people who were skeptical, but as he noted, they believe now.

In 2016 he set up an offshore buying desk in Colombia which only broke even, so he shut it down. Then he learned about Fairmarkit and decided to take a chance on it. This CPO's original logic was that if it brought back 5 percent the investment would be worth it. After 18 months they have saved 15 percent on all transactions sent to Fairmarkit. The criterion to trigger a requisition to go to Fairmarkit is the purchase being under $100,000 and not on a contract. It's a "no-touch" process if that criterion is met. In turn, this has created an SLA turnaround time of anywhere between 24 and 48 hours, which delights his users. Building on the initial success, the CPO has an ambitious agenda to expand this into services moving upstream into engineering, facilities, and IT. Currently the threshold for the sourcing team to take over is $100,000, but he has no doubt that Fairmarkit can easily handle those transactions. For him it's a political issue right now.

They were able to deploy in three weeks. His keys to success include: know what you're doing, take it in bite-size pieces, and build positive experiences and credibility one stakeholder at a time. Once deployed they piloted two categories and restricted who was involved to friendly people. From there he slowly opened it up one stakeholder, department, location at a time. The program has been a financial windfall with virtually no cash outlay. He repeatedly emphasized that you need to know what you're doing and be engaged in the process. He is so involved that he views his partners at Fairmarkit as friends. This of course gives him the right level of access if and when he needs it.

When it comes to digital maturity, the CPO pointed out that he surrounds himself with tech people so that he can learn from them. They teach him how to navigate new tech, open doors to new vendors, new ideas. In return, he helps them by sharing his hard-earned wisdom on how to succeed in (or sell into) the corporate environment. He coaches them on the value of expertise and precise messaging. The relationships become a symbiotic, continuously evolving dynamic.

3.5.4 Globality

What the solution is supposed to do
Globality is a Source-to-SOW platform designed for non-catalogable categories, such as services. Historically, sourcing services has been difficult because every specification is different and business stakeholders have a complex intent that is often incompletely described or specified. The solution, driven by a significant amount of sophisticated machine learning, consists of five parts (scope, match, compare, negotiate, record).

First is an assisted process that effortlessly walks users through creating the scope definition. This phase is where the system intelligence is on full display as it generates contextually relevant and useful prompts to the user. Underpinning this process is a set of cost levers to drive to optimal price outcomes. The platform is continuously learning, capturing observations from every sourcing request, and drawing on millions of data points throughout the sourcing process.

The second and equally compelling part of the solution is immediate access to instantaneous matching with a pre-qualified and actively managed set of suppliers for each category. This includes both the preferred suppliers of each client and an ever-growing (currently 20,000) marketplace of other suppliers who often have SMB or diversity certifications. Quality reigns over quantity. The innovation here is that the platform is using networked intelligence to match the most qualified, capable suppliers to the specific need. This opens the playing field to new/innovative/diverse/SMB suppliers and circumvents the traditional corporate procurement blind spots of lack of choices or lack of interest in finding new qualified suppliers; the solution does that automatically.

Then the platform facilitates a tendering process. Here the goal is to facilitate side-by-side comparisons of the proposals. This part is what makes sourcing services so difficult because every proposal has variations and nuances that make like-for-like comparisons difficult. Globality solves this problem rather elegantly, as it forces suppliers to respond specifically and accurately to the tender (as someone who participates in responding to complex services tenders the irony is not lost on this author).

The fourth element of the platform is a negotiation capability in which all the relevant stakeholders are invited to rate the supplier responses. These ratings in turn are factored back into the matching algorithms described above to make specific award recommendations. Much like Amazon factors ratings and reviews into its recommendations, Globality is doing the same for corporate buying of complex services.

Finally, and perhaps most importantly, the platform takes awarded and accepted supplier proposals and automatically pushes them into the relevant systems of record. Technically Globality can integrate into contract life-cycle management, procure-to-pay, and vendor-management systems. This seamless integration capability ensures that none of the activity conducted on the platform requires human intervention or duplication of work.

How the client uses it
I interviewed two mutual clients for this part. Both use the tool and are quite happy with it. One client uses it to go after long-unaddressed services spend. As they do, they're seeing double-digit savings up and down their services spend. The other client, which is as mature as procurement groups get, has a really good handle on cost. For them, what Globality does in particular is let the business user community use the tool directly so that procurement doesn't need to be in the middle of sourcing activity. This has created very nice efficiency benefits.

3.5.5 Absolute realness: the BT Sourced Digital Procurement Garage[1]

In late 2019, BT Sourced (BTS) created its Digital Procurement Garage (DPG). The DPG offers start-ups a (pre-COVID) place to work, data, and referenceability. In return, BTS gets access to the latest and greatest technology. BTS uses the DPG to augment its brand new S2P implementation to fill in gaps and expand capabilities into areas where its S2P provider isn't focused. Not only was BTS's Digital Procurement Garage one of the coolest innovations of 2020, but it ranks as one of the most successful deployments of technology in procurement history (no exaggeration). Perhaps as much as any of the examples above, BTS has successfully employed a number of innovative start-up technologies. Over the past year, I have personally witnessed Cyril Pourrat (BTS CPO) and Adam Brown (Director of BTS's Digital Procurement Garage) create, innovate, and co-create with a wide variety of technology start-ups.

What's different is that they treat the start-ups as partners instead of vendors. This is in sharp contrast to the normal way of operating, which usually consists of passively waiting for a nearly perfect solution (a red herring to be sure) to be hand-delivered and then poking significant holes in it before going through an arduous system implementation. To put it more succinctly, instead of waiting for a gourmet meal to be served to them, the DPG works to grow, harvest, cook, and eat the meal, which has a far more likelihood of success (and tastes much better).

The benefits of the DPG are both obvious and significant as they get early access to the latest technology. Also, this gives them the ability to shape the technology developments to meet their needs first. More importantly, BTS has become the place where innovators seek to go (technologists, academics, and venture capitalists). It is a magnet that attracts and develops cutting-edge ideas instead of having to seek them out. With this first mover advantage it's not hard to imagine that over time BTS will take an equity stake in some of these start-ups.

---

[1] BT Sourced is a newly established standalone procurement company within the British Telecom Group. For more information see https://newsroom.bt.com/bts-new-procurement-company-bt-sourced-kicks-off-dublin-operations-with-recruitment-drive/.

The implication of the DPG is that it will dramatically change how procurement technology strategies are developed and executed (see figure 21). Instead of developing a three- to five-year static road map that gets updated periodically, the Digital Procurement Garage is a dynamic strategy that is constantly evolving, based on progress. It can adjust as business realities (M&A) or macro disruption. This is a real-world proof point of how technology success can and should be measured in three to six weeks (as opposed to three to six years). In procurement, we have become passive consumers. We just expect the vendor to show up and everything to work. That's how we got into trouble before. You need to show up, not sit back and wait for someone to serve you the magic button. To further prove this point, as this book goes to print a number of enterprises are undertaking similar DPG efforts.

3.6 Open source procurement

The open source movement (OSM) makes software freely available by volunteers and company contributions. Dating back to the late 1990s, and spurred by the Linux operating system and the Netscape web browser, the OSM has become a mainstay for the high-tech community.[2] Nearly all the software that runs the Internet and most enterprises has a surprisingly high number of open source components to it. In recent years this has expanded to include analytics algorithms, and data processing and management technology have become open source too. Uber and Facebook have been at the forefront of this revolution, contributing significantly to the advancement of data science with open-sourced machine learning models, neural network how-tos, object detection, and scaling data ingestion just to name a few.[3] A crucial example is the Android OS, which enables an ecosystem of hardware providers to build smartphones around it. There's no "owner" per se and anybody is free to take the code base and use it for their needs. All modifications to the code base are fully transparent, documented, and auditable—unlike commercial software which is a black box and opaque.

---

[2] "History of the OSI," updated October 2018, https://opensource.org/history
[3] Uber: "Open Source Program Case Studies: Uber," *TODO*, July 7, 2019, https://todogroup.org/blog/why-we-run-an-open-source-program-uber/
Facebook: Justin W. Flory, "A look inside Facebook's open source program," *Opensource.com*, January 2018, https://opensource.com/article/18/1/inside-facebooks-open-source-program

Figure 21
Digital Procurement Garage

	Traditional approach		Future with Digital Procurement Garage
Road map	Multiyear road map developed to address current stakeholder needs		Continuously monitor market for innovative solutions
Onboarding	Lengthy RFP process to evaluate fully baked solutions and invest to customize		Optimize time and cost commitment to get access to cutting-edge solutions
Adoption	Time and resources spent to drive adoption of new tool that involves significant process changes		Bring the business as you go Business stakeholders and users take the life-cycle journey with you

Feedback loop mechanism

| **Scan** | **Engage partner(s)** | **Accelerated codesign** | **Test and learn** | **Scale** |

Source: Kearney analysis

3.6.1 The Procurement Foundry story

The question of what makes a business-related online community successful has so far eluded supply chain/procurement researchers and product developers alike. It's painful to go to an online community only to see nobody there and/or content that's months or years old. If I post a question or comment I want to feel that it's seen and acknowledged. If one posts something and nobody responds, that indicates that nobody is active and diminishes the likelihood of posting again.

People need to feel that their engagement is worth the effort, that they are a part of something bigger than themselves, something that is the hallmark of the OSM. Additionally, there needs to be a good content draw—either access to experts, unique content, or both. A successful online community creates value for its participants, facilitates meaningful interaction, and is about the exchange of thoughts, ideas, and musings with the experts rather than acquiescing to the experts, as is often the case at conferences and webinars. Online communities are not about highly polished and vetted material; it's the raw co-creation of ideas that will organically grow and evolve. In other words, this is not about privileging one class of people over the other; in a community everyone's voice is privileged. For evidence of this, look at the first Procurement Foundry (PF) Forge virtual conference event—it was more of a structured community sharing of insights than a conference.

The PF is an exemplar of the OSM's applicability to procurement. Due to timing, luck, and vision, PF combined OSM principles to unlock the secret of what makes a successful online community. In March/April 2020, the exact moment that the procurement profession needed a central community to share RFI templates, supplier lists, CSR techniques, and of course PPE, the PF was there to freely facilitate this exchange. The PF became the Github, the online repository of open software source code, for procurement.

The PF is not only free to members, but in 2020 members were also offered the opportunity to invest in an initial capital raise. These reasons, and many more, are why the members are fanatical in their engagement and support of the community. It would not be too far-fetched to see people with PF tattoos in the near future.

In September 2019, months before the pandemic would hit, the PF approached me to serve on its board. I readily accepted this invitation as I sensed something special about this initiative, but never did I imagine quite the innovation I would observe. My involvement with the PF has given me a front-row seat to witness how procurement collaboration has gone open source by extending beyond the four walls. This experience has completely and utterly shifted my perspective about what's possible and what the future holds for procurement. The more I witness in PF the deeper my belief in the procurement community at large.

As described by founder Mike Cadieux, Procurement Foundry was

"[o]riginally designed as a small LinkedIn Group, called The Real Deal—the plan was to get 50 sourcing practitioners into a small private group to collaborate and share best practices surrounding in-flight projects, vendor engagements, and negotiations. It was a closed group, and the only way in was by invitation from an existing member. Four months later 50 had grown to 1,100, and we realized LinkedIn Groups wasn't going to cut it. And more importantly there's a huge gap for quality peer engagement opportunities in our industry. So we investigated collaboration platforms and found Slack, [we] rebranded as Procurement Foundry, and opened the front door to any industry buy-side practitioners that wanted access. We are closing in on 4,500 members, with 40 regional chapters, and hosting 200-plus industry events in 2021 alone, ranging from regional meetups to full industry virtual conferences. We're building a safe haven for our practitioners to gather, share, and grow. While we are happy with the early success and growth, we have big plans and a lot more value to add to industry practitioners."

What is notable about PF is that it turns the traditional pay-to-play model on its head. It's free to members. Vendors and consultants are ancillary, constrained to segmented sandboxes. This makes the community pure and free from selling.

The traditional model for industry groups is to charge both vendors and members. The ROI is based on the industry group selling the contact information to the vendors. At face value this doesn't make sense for vendor or member because members are often in discussions with vendors already and can easily contact the vendors themselves. This business model is anachronistic and a bit dishonest. Selling user contact information is a lazy business model. In a truly competitive marketplace, these organizations would create value beyond selling contact information. And yet this has been the standard modus operandi for all industry groups. The other thing that COVID-19 exposed is the fragility of these organizations to create value beyond the in-person conference. Increasingly I hear that the benefit of these in-person conferences is that they are a chance to get out of the office and do a bit of networking. Ideally, and perhaps once upon a time, these conferences should have provided unique and differentiated insights and robust networking opportunities. Yet they have atrophied and are shells of their former selves. They seem to exist as a means to their survival instead of providing tangible value. When you dig deeper into the content you find that much of it is regurgitated and old. These organizations should exist to push the boundaries and facilitate transformative topics. In other words, would anybody notice or care if these organizations went away?

I say this as someone who thrives on speaking to a live audience. Unless industry groups evolve quickly they risk complete and total obsolescence. If it's not too late already.

3.6.2 Going further

The significance of procurement open source is the opportunity to move some purchasing and contracting activities outside the four walls. Open source, technology-enabled group purchasing capabilities are the most obvious next step whereby companies can easily participate in group-buying exchanges. With the sophistication of technology, these events can be executed with very little operational overhead. But open-source concepts can extend to employee development and external collaboration. The most prolific and public example of this occurred between IKEA, Maersk, and HSBC. These three companies exchanged two procurement employees for six-month stints—the benefits of which are many, including individual skill development and shared organizational learnings.[4]

Moving beyond the limitation of the four walls opens up completely new ways of ensuring supply. Community interactions open up new ways of purchasing and collaborating. If you have 5,000 procurement practitioners collaborating with one another, open-source options include the sharing of other types of sophisticated and seemingly commoditized intellectual capital. From there it's not hard to imagine group purchasing from the community.

At the risk of being a generational determinist, Boomers built most procurement organizations and best practices. These were all about sharing nothing outside the four walls. Information was exchanged, at least in theory, at industry conferences and through consultants and industry organizations that worked across clients and built benchmarks. Plus, the Boomer generation tended to move jobs infrequently. But in the Facebook and Wikileaks era that feels anachronistic. Millennials share everything and tend to work at many different places. Gen Xers are stuck in the middle, schizophrenically trying to mediate between the two. Recognizing that sharing is a core component of this generation and inevitable, why not embrace it now? This exemplifies the epitome of networking and learning from others, something that has been extremely limited to date.

Building a "community" is not a technology problem. It's enabled by technology, but the bulk of community building is done by someone with charisma, timing, perseverance, building buzz, sustaining, and tapping into a collective need. "If you build it they'll come" doesn't work. This is about building one-on-one relationships, getting people excited, and facilitating sharing, a collectivist approach where people feel compelled to donate their time, expertise, and provide mentorship. Collaboration cannot be bought or forced.

---

[4] Tom Graham, "Creating the 360 Procurement professional: The HSBC, Maersk & IKEA exchange programme," Berkwith Partners, January 23, 2020, https://www.berwickpartners.co.uk/what-we-think/leadership-insights/creating-the-360-procurement-professional-the-hsbc-maersk-ikea-exchange-programme-12567/

3.7 Implications

We have seen not only a new digital model for procurement, but also a user-friendly way to get there. Your journey toward digital procurement is exciting because it's transformational. But it's never finished.

3.7.1 Processes

Why do we set a process, a "best-in-class" process, and then walk away as if the job is done? In today's world, full of massive macro disruptions (pandemics, trade wars, populism) and rapidly shifting business realities (acquisitions/divestitures, market expansion/contraction), how can any process be static? This is a recipe for being flat-footed in response to a crisis (as happened to most companies with COVID-19).

To put it another way, what is the process to improve the process? After all, in this global reality, there can no longer be a single, permanent "best-in-class." That is an anachronistic idea, like a single ERP system. It may have worked in decades past, but it no longer works today. For example, a "best practice" is to have a PO with several levels of approvals based on spending thresholds. But in a crisis when you need to negotiate rates/variances/payment terms on the fly, there have to be accelerated controls and thresholds in place to quickly respond. If a supplier loses a crucial manufacturing facility because of a natural disaster (and assuming you haven't adequately distributed risk), how quickly can you onboard a new supplier, even if prices will be higher than the approved threshold? This is what it means to operate in an agile manner. We cannot predict everything that will happen and our best-laid plans may not be feasible, so we need to be able to have the flexibility, driven by superb information, to react to the unknown in a nimble way. If "best-in-class" spend control is the goal, just automate those controls and fire the procurement team. Controlling spending is a pedantic task and doesn't require significant resources.

This gets to a broader cultural reality: so many businesses are operating in a post-WWII mindset in which employees can't be trusted and need to be controlled. But in an era of hyper-transparency and sophisticated technology, that legacy mindset isn't helping. It's actually hurting. Why not move to a trust-but-verify mindset, a concept popularized by American President Ronald Reagan during the nuclear arms negotiations with the Soviet Union during the 1980s? Reagan's premise is applicable here, whereby you implicitly trust people to do the right thing and enable them to do so. Among the significant operating model changes emanating from Silicon Valley over the past two decades, perhaps the least appreciated is the adoption of the trust-but-verify mindset. Google, Netflix, Amazon, and others trust their users to use data by giving them direct access to it, which spurs many of the productivity gains and innovations.

This is unlike traditional organizations that hide data away in hard-to-access silos that require fourteen levels of approval and six months of haggling.

Innovative companies have taken this trend into concepts such as IT vending machines. Just as it sounds, this is a vending machine full of all kinds of IT accessories (earpods, iPad cases, mice, and so on), free to any employee. They simply scan and go. This is the pinnacle of efficiency; it's fully transparent and anyone who abuses the system will stand out. Basically, you're enabling the 99 percent instead of constraining them because of a few bad apples. Moreover, there's no need for procurement to be involved because the vending machine can communicate directly with the supplier that fills it. A seamless and elegant no-touch process. Also, as it tracks consumption data over time, it can provide demand forecasting capabilities.

Further, the work-from-home (WFH) model, something most organizations were thrust into, is based on the trust-but-verify concept. Why not implicitly trust employees to permanently work from home in a fully digital manner? Who cares if someone drives their kid to school, does some laundry, or takes a walk during the day? All we should care about is whether the work is getting done when it needs to be done. Initial anecdotal data from this crisis points to the fact that many people are working harder from home. Of course, this may have implications for what the new model will be: less travel, reductions in real-estate footprint, less facilities management, and even the need for more proactive network security on home networks.

But to enable this move to digital operations, we need the proper digital tools. We're asking people to use data, be analytically minded, be digital, continuously learn, and be creative. And somehow IT groups are magically tasked with figuring this out for every employee. People learn in different ways. People create in different ways. People find joy in different ways. So why is IT emboldened to force a standard set of tools upon us? Why are they gatekeepers of perceived productivity? How can they know me, my learning style, what will make me successful? Nor should they be required to.

Plus, if WFH is enabling a change in how we work, then we need to look beyond the idea that the primary device is a laptop. Perhaps we need to consider that the phone or tablet is the most productive (if not secure) device for working from home. This means that the core set of productivity apps has to be reimagined. This means that peripherals have to be rethought. Maybe home projectors, headphones, good microphones (not just headsets), even backgrounds (physical and virtual) need to be considered. Undoubtedly HR will have to develop new guidelines for what is and is not acceptable in the background. Perhaps IT's role should be to focus on the platform/OS and let users use the individual apps of their choice. All of this points to the criticality for the extensible procurement platform to enable this new way of working.

I understand the need for security and complexity reduction, but perhaps we have over-indexed on uniformity versus enablement. It's like how before COVID the focus was solely on cost versus risk, an imbalance that was catastrophically out of kilter. One could argue that before COVID IT over-indexed on ease of management over productivity enablement.

Armed with these digital tools, we need to embrace digital ways of working. This is not adapting our in-person processes to digital tools, but instead figuring out how to use these tools and how to truly unlock their power. What are the rules? How do we govern? How do we avoid duplicating work? More importantly, how we share is different. Ever since Napster hit the market the concept of sharing has taken on a whole new concept whereby if it's a digital file it's easy—if not expected—to be shared. Facebook furthered this dynamic by getting all of us to willingly share our entire life stories, likes/dislikes, and deepest darkest secrets. Spotify, Pandora, Netflix, and Hulu ushered in on-demand whereby everything is at our fingertips.

These are new digital literacies (see figure 22). The figure shows the evolution of digital literacies and the implications for the digital tools that support them. This will foreshadow how additional consumer-facing technologies will

Figure 22
Evolution of digital literacies

Boomer	Gen X	Millennial/Gen Y
"Email the doc"	"It's on Slack"	"What's a document?"
"Call me"	"Text me"	"@me"
"Here's the PPT"	"Why are we still using PPT?"	"Where's the meme?"
"Heard it at the watercooler"	"Read it on Facebook"	"Heard it on Clubhouse"

Source: Kearney analysis

continue to influence the corporate computing environment. For example, TikTok is not about dancing and middle-aged men trying to impress their daughters, but rather a new way of conveying and understanding emotional connections. Not only by the creator, but also by the audience that's viewing, responding, and reflecting the message back. Similarly, YouTube, iTunes, Instagram, and Medium are places where influencers are born. These creators make millions of dollars performing (drumming, comedy, singing, and so on), doing tutorials, or simply unboxing products. Of course, the biggest market is gamers who livestream their exploits on Twitch. There are no rules, no bosses, and the growth is completely organic. These people use iPads, fancy mics, greenscreens, and a whole host of other technology to produce multimillion-dollar broadcasts. Imagine trying to explain to one of these people how to do a requisition at a Fortune 500 company. Talk about the Mars versus Venus dynamic.

The business world is still coming to terms with all these developments.

3.7.2 Using technology for knowledge management

Frequently I'm asked, "What's the best knowledge management system for procurement?" or "How do I effectively capture our procurement knowledge?" First off, knowledge cannot be "managed." It can however be shared. Perhaps the more relevant question is, "How do we use technology to improve our procurement interactions and relationships?" The right mechanisms (tools and incentives) have to be in place. But before that, we need to look at every activity and determine if we can codify it, meaning is there a pattern to it? If there's any kind of pattern, then it can be codified and eventually automated. Moreover, the idea of "best-in-class" templates is anachronistic and just a tiny bit narcissistic. The codification of activity should come from what's happening in the systems. Here we need to get the technology providers to take a more active role. Vendors serving multiple clients have the ability to mine activity across clients and deduce what options and techniques lead to the greatest savings. Basically, the activity within a particular tool holds patterns of what works and what doesn't. This means that templates can be democratized and ideally embedded in the tools. And they don't even have to be branded to a particular organization. In essence, templates become part of the public good.

Once we detect the pattern we can start to automate portions of it. Hence the reason buying desks, sourcing activities, and even some category/commodity management will become increasingly automated. It's the inevitable outcome; the only question is how long it will take and how to effectively do it for each organization.

3.7.3 New talent

Assuming all this new-fangled technology comes to pass, it's clear that companies will need talent with a whole set of new skills. Procurement professionals of the future will need far different traits than they have today. (University programs and industry groups need to change as well.)

Procurement organizations need people who can think creatively, who look beyond a single tower or issue. They must be technologically savvy and comfortable with analytics. Historically, and even still today, employees struggle with technology systems, basic digital security, and analytics. This is partly a generational thing, but even Millennials and younger generations have their own blind spots. Next-generation procurement practitioners need to be able to think in the context of both bottom line, top-line impact and the business impact in the broader market. There is, and increasingly will continue to be, a direct line from procurement to consumer. So issues such as supply disruptions, ingredients, and quality should factor ever more into each person's performance. Today these issues are too disconnected, if indeed they are even examined.

On top of that, professionals will need a deeper concentration in digital operations, demand, and SRM capabilities. For digital operations, most organizations have the equivalent of half an FTE focused on managing the S2P provider contract. That is not digital. That will not get it done in the modern era. There needs to be a team of folks looking after the procurement digital stack. They need to be continually evaluating the effectiveness and usage of procurement's tools, looking for problem spots and inefficiencies, to proactively fix them. The good news is that there's a whole host of tools that will surface these issues so they can be addressed. In other words, don't wait for the user to make the complaint, because if you wait until that point, the reputation damage will be ten times worse. Digital operations might be done in concert with IT, especially for very specialized capabilities such as data scientist, data engineer, or product architect. Procurement needs to be able to articulate its needs to IT. And, if/when IT shows intransigence, the digital operations folks need to address the concerns and come up with the right solution.

We no longer need to hire category managers with decades of experience. That expertise is a commodity. Between tools, insights (benchmarks, price indexes, and so on), and supply markets, what a category manager does is changing. As we make category managers more efficient, we can start to collapse the number of category managers required. Those that remain should specialize in their knowledge and have a deeper capability to deliver value in negotiations, IP protection, and joint-process improvement. All of which is spurred by and effectively managed by digital procurement.

It's common to make fun of consultants; they come in and listen to all your ideas then simply play them back to the senior leaders while charging hundreds of thousands of dollars. And yet, if you ask executives what kind of skills and experience they are looking to hire, it sounds exactly like the skills consultants possess. Essentially, clients are looking to hire people with the profiles of consultants, but at a fraction of the price (and perhaps with less emotional baggage). These skills include:

— **Business athlete.** The ability to understand trade-offs, constraints, ROI, and generally the factors and theories of running a business. This skillset allows thinking beyond one's individual function, which comes in handy for writing business cases.

— **Motivation.** The world is changing all the time. The business landscape is continually changing too. Digital tools and techniques are continually changing. This means that learning is a continual process. Learning comes down to one thing: motivation. You can provide a user with all the online or in-person classes they want, but if they aren't motivated, they won't learn.

— **Digital.** Wanting, embracing, and exploring technology. Not afraid to make mistakes with technology. Able to consider how technology could improve operations.

— **Analytically minded and data driven.** If given data, this person should be able to quickly sift through, interpret, and analyze into insights.

— **Emotional intelligence.** The smartest person in the room rarely comes out on top. The problem with super-smart people is that they are annoyed by those who aren't as smart as them. The ones who succeed have patience and the ability to read other people's emotions. Despite the intense focus on digital, much of what is argued herein is about relationship-building. Cultivating relationships is a human experience and the sum total of interactions, which can often be a give and take.

— **Creativity.** The old adage of "thinking outside the box" is so clichéd. In fact, we do so much thinking that does not reside in a box that one wonders if there are a bunch of empty boxes. The takeaway here is that following a script or a playbook is no longer useful. The reality of the world and business environment we operate in these days doesn't fit into a nice simple framework or playbook.

— **Problem life cycle management.** Treat problems like there's no other option than to create a solution for the problem. Identifying problems and raising the alarm is no different than being an order-taker. We need to move to where we identify the problem, create solutions, test their likelihood of success, and either solve the problem or seek guidance/approval.

— **Advanced communication.** The ability to write in long form (Word) and short form (PPT). The skills are dramatically different, yet equally important. Long-form writing in the business context, being able to build an effective business case based on establishing a hypothesis, data, and analysis. For example, should we spin our procurement organization into a separate company? This is where the heavy-duty supporting and counterarguments need to be spelled out. By contrast, short-form writing (PPT) is the synthesis of the analysis and/or messages you want to convey. This is where every word choice matters. The litmus test of good PPT is to extract the text from it and read it out loud. That's when you see really bad short-form writing.

— **Superb presentation skills.** The ability to tell a good story that is anchored in deep expertise is crucial. Humans respond well to storytelling so cultivating those skills is vital. Giving enough detail without being too superficial but not burying people with too much.

— **Executive presence.** Presenting to and interacting with executives should not be a shock. Junior folks should cultivate this skill early and often. It's a cliché to say that executives are just like you and me, but it's true. What's different is their time and their cues. When we say executive presence we mean have you learned how to read the cues? I am no longer intimidated by executives. I hold them in high regard, but I no longer fear them. They are human just like you and me. They have wants, dreams, and desires.

— **Building respect/reputation.** Today everyone needs a personal brand. This is for both internal and external purposes. People need to think about their careers in multidimensions.

— **Synthesize for a multiplicity of audiences.** In the course of a given day consultants need to be able to deliver key information to people across the enterprise. The first meeting might be to workers on the manufacturing plant floor. Then the next meeting might be to the company's CEO and board. The ability to quickly and flexibly convey messages for dramatically different audiences is crucial to success as a consultant.

This transformation in hiring criteria may not be as hard to implement as it sounds. The raw talent graduating from undergrad and MBA programs is staggering. Curriculums have changed dramatically over the past decade. Business analytics, and in some cases data science, is much more of a priority. Those newly minted MBAs have skills that make for a very strong core upon which to build independent thinking along with a hyper-focused ability to manage the full life cycle of projects. Add a comfort level in technology, and the desire to improve and innovate, and that is what the future (in some cases current) procurement person should look like.

It's important to hire these incredibly talented people because tomorrow's digitally enabled procurement function will be about having a high-performing team with specialized skills working together to tackle the strategic needs of the enterprise—needs that will become even more crucial as the global economy continues to be shaken by political upheaval and changing demographics.

This approach will strengthen the reputation of the procurement function as a collection of value-adding partners who will improve the overall perceptions of the profession. It will also create opportunities to define varied career paths that can better connect with the business, particularly for the product or service and commodity roles. Thus, the path to becoming a successful business professional will begin with working on a high-performing procurement team. Whether the individual's final destination is finance, product development, sales, or operations, there's no better place to begin than with creating value for the enterprise by strategically influencing the spend.

3.7.4 Where procurement creates traditional value and why digital is eviscerating it

Perhaps the greatest difference the digital revolution will bring is the move away from cost savings as the singular measure of the value of procurement. First, if the corporate goal is 10 percent annual savings on external spend each year, what happens when digital tools deliver that automatically with no procurement intervention? Second, the value of procurement is its ability to bring the right suppliers to bear at the right time. What happens when digital systems intelligently select the right supplier at the right place and at the right time? What happens when we can deliver today's value with 30 percent of the cost? What will all of us procurement people do?

This is our opportunity to pursue advanced cost strategies, support innovation through third-party orchestration, advance the CSR agenda, and be proactive on risk. Ideally over time, procurement will move from cost center to profit center (or at least cost neutral with a P&L).

3.7.5 The broader context (supply chain and ERP systems)

It's important to see procurement in the broader supply chain and operational context. Current supply chain systems are wholly inadequate to support today's complex, global, and rapidly changing business environment. ERP upgrades or consolidations are choking the life out of businesses. Most existing systems are expensive, slow, and lack the ability to do what truly matters. Innovation is limited and they severely lack flexibility. In short, they are testaments to a different time and place. This section will cover how we got here, why we need to fundamentally change our approach, and what we can do in the near and long term.

Today, supply chains run on software that was designed in the late 1990s. ERPs were new and innovative before 2000—and they have yet to measurably change. Of course, business has changed dramatically in that time. Large enterprises, especially those that grow through acquisition, are far more complex than they used to be. Consumers expect more, businesses need to operate more efficiently, there's greater government regulation, increased competition (where your suppliers often become your competitors), and general supply disruptions (war, tariffs, natural disasters, pandemics, and the like).

In other words, future considerations aside, to operate effectively in today's business environment, you must be nimble. And yet, most enterprises have massive technical debt, in which past shortcuts are hindering current productivity. It's not uncommon to see enterprises with 20, 30, 40, or 100 ERP systems. That is beyond asinine. That is no way to run a business and it certainly wasn't how ERP systems were designed. Of course, it harms attempts at data management, end-to-end visibility, and planning. Sadly, most companies can't see a way out of this mess, so they keep buying and spending more and more money on these failed systems. Even the newest ERP implementations are destined to fail because nobody is taking the long view. There's far too much short-term thinking.

At most large companies with a proliferation of ERP systems, many parties are invested in the status quo. If you have more than 10 ERP systems and you lack basic end-to-end supply chain visibility, you are hampering everything from inventory levels to ability to deliver. Your natural inclination thus may be to undertake an ERP consolidation and harmonization program. That seems logical: reduce the complexity to a single system or at least a manageable set of systems.

But this approach is slow, costly, and in some cases not technically feasible. These consolidation projects perpetuate the status quo and actually hinder efforts to become digital. In fact, these projects are so large and so complex that they make good hiding places for poor or mediocre performers. Even high performers end up falling into complacency under the harness of rigid project management. And that's the best case. The worst case is a form of territorialism that drags the project into cost- and time-delayed oblivion.

Today, we have access to data and analytics that can create, streamline, and automate highly optimized supply chains. But employing these innovations on top of today's technology is often impossible and at best suboptimal. Nevertheless, there's a clear path forward:

1 Over the next 30 years, we need to move beyond the ERP system. In fact, we need to blow up the ERP system and start over (a topic for my next book). In some ways this is what Amazon has done over the past 20 years. Its system is not without issues and is not sustainable for most enterprises, but that points directionally to where things have to go.

2 We need to build autonomous supply chain systems. If we look at the standard plan/source/make/deliver towers, humans should not be doing planning, because machines do it better. And for that matter, machines already do many manufacturing activities and eventually will do the sourcing and delivery better than humans. This does not mean humans go away; instead they take on much more strategic and advisory functions.

3 Supply chains need to be more local. We have spent time, effort, and money building global supply chain systems, but technology (3D printing, pop-up manufacturing, biotech, and so on) is eviscerating that way of operating. In the future, we need to enable a very micro way of operating supply chains. The obvious examples are, if you are a medical device provider, you shouldn't need to design a product in New Jersey, manufacture it in China, and ship it to a surgery center in Chicago. Why not just 3D print it in the surgery center? You shouldn't need to grow food in South America and ship it to Europe—you should be able to grow it locally with biotech augmentation. Furthermore, many products are going natively digital. Think about software: it used to be printed on CDs (or even floppy disks), boxed, shrink-wrapped, and sold in stores. Now it's all digital. This trend is accelerating as our smartphones expand to cover health, finance, and commerce, which will further eliminate the need for physical products and traditional supply chains.

In short, plan/source/make/deliver will soon be replaced by an intelligence layer that sits on top of transactional systems that enable companies to have the necessary end-to-end view for operating agile supply chains (see figure 23 on page 146). So instead of building point-to-point integration between transaction systems, as has been attempted and which failed miserably, we simply offload the relevant data into the intelligence layer which can quickly create the necessary intelligence and distribute it to where it needs to go, whether it's disseminating updated forecast information to suppliers or simply showing a delivery eta to the customer (see sidebar on page 147: How to think about directs in digital procurement).

Figure 23
The supply chain landscape

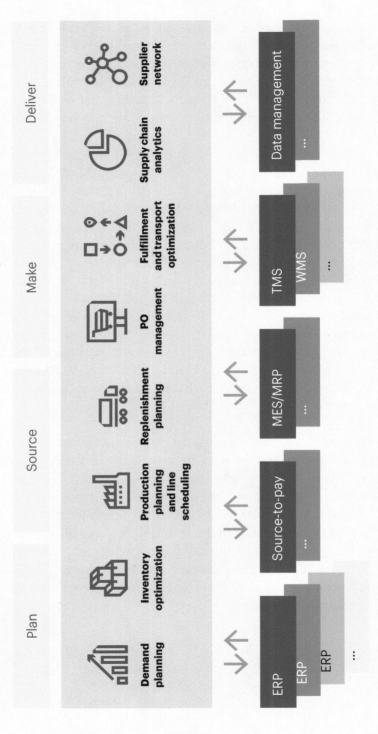

Note: MES = manufacturing execution system, MRP = material requirements planning, TMS = transportation management system, and WMS = warehouse management system.

Source: Kearney analysis

How to think about directs in digital procurement

"But what about directs, what do I do with all these ERP systems?" Questions like this come up at lot. However, the answer is clear. The first phase of digital procurement includes several key capabilities you need that can underpin with any number of ERP systems. You can syndicate supplier records (ideally using a data foundation) to all ERP systems, so that you consolidate around a single source of truth for suppliers. Next, you can offload payments to a central P2P system. This gives you a single, logical place to manage payments, which makes fraud detection, dynamic discounting, and supply chain financing much easier. At the next level, you will tie quality and quantity measures automatically into the contract-to-pay process.

Beyond those capabilities, we need to look at integrating dynamic sourcing into ERP processes. This shouldn't be done within ERPs but should be a function and capability sitting in the supply chain intelligence layer. Sourcing has to be done well in advance of day-to-day operations, which is why having accurate forecasts can open up more flexibility and near-real-time sourcing. Looking upstream, we need to have specifications and bill of materials management. Without them, we face a major impediment to success and future growth. Finally, we need the ability to provide to look downstream and have greater data transparency and integrations with our contract manufacturers (CM) and transportation systems. Who has better commodity pricing? If we do, then is the CM using it? How are we tracking the sourcing of our transportation spend? What this section demonstrates is that we need to move away from the rigid plan/source/make/deliver towers. As seen above, this creates unhelpful data and technology silos that have to be broken down (by an intelligence layer). But this old paradigm also creates a complacency whereby people (whether employees, consultants, analysts, and tech providers) in each tower do not collaborate with one another. I am always puzzled by the quizzical looks and dismissive comments people give me when I suggest that for procurement to be effective we must embed further upstream into planning and downstream into manufacturing. Yet what I hear is, "I don't know anything about planning" or "I have no idea what they do." Failure to move beyond our individual towers will not only continue to limit our effectiveness, but it will also set us up to be displaced by technology.

Section IV
Conclusion

4.1 What's the next disruption?

The COVID-19 crisis will leave its imprint on the operations community for decades. Going forward, risk models, processes, and capabilities will be measured against a potential pandemic. And rightly so. But we must avoid fixating on what's in the rearview mirror. We must also look forward at what could come or is likely to hit us. What will be the next major disruption? What would we do in the event of a massive cyberattack that put large portions of the Internet out of commission? What about a semi-regional nuclear detonation? Or even a larger military conflagration? How about a massive natural disaster that affects multiple geographies?

As a futurist, I have the duty of asking some complicated questions. When making a sourcing award decision, are we factoring concentration of risk into the allocation distribution? Should we trade dollars for carbon impact? How do we negotiate with a supplier who is also a customer where award could impact revenue? Is there a model where bartering and/or shared services could replace currency? These are the questions that procurement could and should be considering as we go forward. All these create tremendous value for an enterprise but have nothing to do with cost savings.

4.2 The CPO tipping point

When I talk to people—and remember, I talk to a *lot* of people—everyone wants to know if we have hit the procurement tipping point.

My response is always the same: "If now is not our moment, then when will it come?" Supply assurance, cost savings, and ESG have never been greater opportunities. Since 2019, procurement has been forced to respond to continued populism, trade wars, a global pandemic, social unrest, and a steady acknowledgement that businesses have to play a key role in addressing global climate change. These are all supply chain and procurement issues. They have nothing to do with sales and marketing. So as a procurement function, if we can't deliver now, then what are we waiting for?

I am heartened to work with a new generation of CPOs. These CPOs are stepping up to the challenge. They are looking beyond chasing fictional cost savings and perpetuating failed "best practice" strategies. Each of them is refusing to accept the status quo. They are the captains of their ships, employing severe critical thinking to their as-is and future direction, even in the face of difficult internal headwinds. Smart transformation is at the top of their agenda. They realize they'll get only one shot at this, and they aren't going waste it. They avoid the big-sunk-cost technology. They demonstrate to the business why they belong at the table—and more to the point are vital contributors. They are shedding the shadow budget control moniker and are focused on enablement. It's a data-driven, high-quality-service approach. They recognize that it's not a least-common-denominator discussion.

The change is not generational. Although a new generation of younger CPOs is leading this charge, equally a number of seasoned CPOs recognize the gravity of today and are eager to make their mark.

There's a saying, "No CIO gets fired for choosing IBM." Although it's a bit out of date, its central insight—that the least-risky choice is the huge vendor with the buttoned-up sales team—has influenced many CIOs and IT organizations. In supply chain and procurement systems, that old saying has mutated to "No CPO gets fired for choosing SAP or Oracle." On the surface, this statement is true. Many a CPO has chosen SAP or Oracle and not been fired for that decision. But maybe that's because CPOs who choose SAP or Oracle, like CIOs who choose IBM, either leave before they get fired or bury themselves in complexity that makes it impossible to fire them. In either case, their behavior impairs the enterprise.

Is the choice a risky one for the CPO? Of course it is. It must hold up to the scrutiny of the CFO and CEO as they release the tens of millions or hundreds of millions of dollars to implement these systems. In such a situation, it's tempting to build a business case chock-full of analysts' recommendations, consultant-validated business cases, and overly invested IT groups. But all these entities are biased. The analysts survive by perpetuating the status quo, the consultants benefit by recommending the systems they'll implement (often in partnership with the system providers), and the IT groups are treated to golf trips, fancy dinners, and luxury "user conferences." When put to the test (pandemic, trade war, supplier diversity, and suchlike), these systems fail to deliver the promised capabilities, insights, and data. At this point, the CPO is an emperor strutting around the office without clothes.

I have made my career by coming in on the heels of failed source-to-pay implementations. Usually, I am brought in by a new CPO. One of the most immediate problems I find is that the benefits were vastly overstated and undelivered—not even rationally achievable. It has always seemed to me that the CPOs who sign up for these systems leave before that decision can be challenged. True, they weren't fired for choosing SAP or Oracle, but they never achieved their visions either. They just slunk off in the night.

People who resist this message often have an overriding belief that "SAP Hana will solve it" or "IBM Watson has that capability." SAP Hana and IBM Watson may or may not be good products, but it's undeniable that nobody really knows what they do. Get 10 procurement people in a room and ask them what either of those products does, and you'll get 10 different answers. This is not a good sign for a procurement system. There is no magic button. Belief in SAP Hana or IBM Watson is belief that a magic button is just around the corner. But any vendor or consultant who cannot clearly articulate what business problem they are solving is not worth investing in, much less betting your career on.

4.3 Watch-outs

There are several predictors of failure in your digital initiatives. If you hear or see these in action, look for imminent failure.

— **It requires lots of training.** This means that whatever it is, it's too complex. It's destined for failure. People don't need to be taught how to use Google, Facebook, or Amazon, so why should we spend hundreds of thousands of dollars on "training" programs for technology solutions?

— **It's a feature masquerading as a product.** There are some innovations that are great ideas but not great as independent solutions. When evaluating new start-ups, ask yourself, "Is this a feature or a product?"[1]

— **Your middle managers.** Middle managers, especially those closer to retirement, are the biggest impediments to digital success. Their endgame is self-preservation, making them risk averse. These people engage in what can be termed empty calorie management—they overcomplicate initiatives to create job security. They're easy to spot because they are known for generating a lot of activity (calls, meetings, emails, and so on) but showing very little productivity. Their incentive lies with extending projects, creating long milestones, and expanding project scopes, rather than driving rapid returns on tangible, measurable projects.

— **Organizational turnover.** Turnover is normal in large enterprises, but it's deadly for big S2P (and ERP) projects. The problem with turnover during these implementations is that the key stakeholders and even sponsors often leave. This creates a gap in the project oversight that allows for excuses to seep in because the tech vendor becomes the proverbial fox in the hen house. When vendors are left unchecked, they can blame any issues that arise on the organizational turnover. Plus, usually the new people coming into the job will want to put their stamp on the project, which means change orders, time delays, and cost overruns.

— **Trigger words.** "Closed loop," "survey," or an abundance of buzzwords (AI, blockchain, RPA, machine learning, IoT, predictive analytics). These words attempt to confer a level of sophistication by means of a lazy shortcut. It doesn't work.

[1] Credit goes to entrepreneur Joel Hyatt, Stanford Business School lecturer and Globality founder, for this insight.

You must demand **no more excuses**—not from your people, not from the vendors, not from the analysts, and definitely not from the consultants.

4.4 How do we know we succeeded?

We will know we succeeded when procurement methods are invisible to the end users. Digital procurement done well will optimize cost, reduce risk, drive innovation, and advance ESG efforts at scale. As a function we must be willing and able to orchestrate this. This is our opportunity if not imperative. More bluntly, if we're not doing this, then what are we actually doing other than waiting to be disrupted?

To truly be digital we must be able to answer the following questions in the affirmative:

— Do we have a handle on our spend?

— Have we stopped using Excel as the default tool?

— Have we stopped using humans to cut and paste data from one system to another?

— Have we stopped spending tens of millions of dollars on a single closed-loop vendor?

— Have we enabled automatic cost savings on our transactional spend?

— Are we using our spend to drive our enterprise ESG goals?

— Are we enabling innovation with our digital capability?

— Are we enabling delightful interactions with the business?

— Are we avoiding risk, and is our crisis response helpful or obstructive?

To execute a digital procurement strategy, we must be able to answer the following questions in the affirmative:

— Did we successfully deliver the promised benefits to the business?

— Did we engage the business sufficiently to identify all the gaps and opportunities?

— Did we effectively balance addressing the tactical issues of today versus building the strategic capabilities of tomorrow?

— Did we deliver within a meaningful timeline?

— Did our efforts at change management bring everyone on the journey with us?

4.5 This is our journey

Call this book a manifesto, an aspiration, or even a dream. Maybe I'm right, maybe I'm wrong, I'm a futurist after all; being wrong is in the job description. What I am reflecting is a deep dissatisfaction from customers of the procurement technology market. I have heard very clearly that procurement practitioners, the business stakeholders they serve, and even some who work for the technology providers themselves is that we can and must do better. We have to move on from the past. We have to imagine a new future—one in which the way we operate is vastly simpler and personalized. We need to challenge the existing logic of rigidly standardized business processes that were designed in a different era. Fear of complexity cannot drive us. Responses to the pandemic have shown us how far we can change and how quickly. We need to move beyond cost savings as the guiding principle for what we do.

My premise is simple: if it adds value, do more of it; if it's complicated, then question it, robustly. I work in a particular space in the market focused on start-ups. I wrestle with the question of why there is so much VC money in procurement (and supply chain). Or, why did Workday acquire Scout for $540 million? These trends are significant and represent a vast departure from the past. To be sure, procurement start-ups are not a panacea. Some start-ups will go out of business, others will get acquired, and some will go public. All will eventually raise their prices. But the ones that succeed have the ability to create extraordinary value.

By now it's obvious that macro disruptions are part of doing business in a globalized world. It's no longer about black swan once-in-a-generation events, but rather a never-ending series of grey swan (not-so-improbable) events. The true measure of our ability to operate digitally, whether from home or in the office, will be our ability to change processes on the fly. In the midst of the next global crisis, can we talk to our suppliers and if we see a need, change payment terms, extend emergency funds, or even do a joint investment with other companies to support the supplier? Can we do that quickly, effectively, and efficiently? We need to get away from rigidly defined teams and toward more flexible teams that can be directed at hot spots. This is dependent on our ability to stop fooling around chasing or fulfilling procurement requests, haggling over small contracts, or pursuing phantom savings.

We must let go of the past. (Star Wars fans may recall Kylo Ren in *The Last Jedi*: "Let the past die. Kill it, if you have to.") It's not about "serving" or "partnering" with the business. We *are* the business. That requires a cultural change. We must have a bias for action. If that means sidestepping the ERP, making tough decisions about the future, and making bold choices, then that's the only way we will become what we are meant to be.

In short, we need to be vastly more efficient, move beyond Excel. We need to stop throwing people and processes at the next crisis to make up for technology's failures. We need to stop being a shadow budgetary control function. Instead, digital can turn procurement into the most mature, intelligent, and exciting function in the enterprise. In the process, we can be part of the solution to society's greatest problems. Now is our time to meet the moment.

CPSIA information can be obtained
at www.ICGtesting.com
Printed in the USA
LVHW021956290721
693999LV00005B/16/J